For an Ecology of Images

Peter Szendy is David Herlihy Professor of Humanities and Comparative Literature at Brown University. His many books include *The Supermarket of the Visible*; *Hits: Philosophy in the Jukebox*; *Kant in the Land of Extraterrestrials*; and *All Ears: The Aesthetics of Espionage.*

Translator Marco Roth is a cofounder of *n+1* and the author of *The Scientists: A Family Romance.*

For an Ecology of Images

Peter Szendy

Translated by Marco Roth

VERSO
London · New York

Albertine Translation

This work received support for excellence in publication and translation from Albertine Translation, formerly French Voices, a program created by Villa Albertine.

This English-language edition first published by Verso 2025

First published as *Pour une écologie des images*

1 3 5 7 9 10 8 6 4 2

Verso
UK: 6 Meard Street, London W1F 0EG
US: 207 East 32nd Street, New York, NY 10016
versobooks.com

Verso is the imprint of New Left Books

ISBN-13: 978-1-80429-431-4
ISBN-13: 978-1-80429-432-1 (UK EBK)
ISBN-13: 978-1-80429-433-8 (US EBK)

British Library Cataloguing in Publication Data
A catalogue record for this book is available from the British Library

Library of Congress Cataloging-in-Publication Data

Names: Szendy, Peter, author. | Roth, Marco, 1974- translator.
Title: For an ecology of images / Peter Szendy ; translated by Marco Roth.
Other titles: Pour une écologie des images. English
Description: London ; New York : Verso, 2025. | Translation of: Pour une écologie des images. | Includes bibliographical references.
Identifiers: LCCN 2024038187 (print) | LCCN 2024038188 (ebook) | ISBN 9781804294314 (trade paperback) | ISBN 9781804294321 (UK EBK) | ISBN 9781804294338 (US EBK)
Subjects: LCSH: Image (Philosophy) | Aesthetics. | Art—Philosophy.
Classification: LCC BH301.I52 S9413 2025 (print) | LCC BH301.I52 (ebook) | DDC 111/.85—dc23/eng/20240919
LC record available at https://lccn.loc.gov/2024038187
LC ebook record available at https://lccn.loc.gov/2024038188

Typeset in Sabon by MJ & N Gavan, Truro, Cornwall
Printed and bound by CPI Group (UK) Ltd, Croydon, CR0 4YY

Contents

Prelude
(In Memory of Imre Kinszki)

I would like to dedicate the following reflections to the memory of my great-uncle, Imre Kinszki.[1]

We called him *Imre bácsi*, "uncle Imre."

I wonder sometimes what Imre bácsi would have thought about the billions upon billions of photographs that are posted and circulated each day on social media networks. I wonder what he would have made of this unprecedented and immeasurable change of scale in the regime of the image's existence.

Imre Kinszki was a photographer, a little less famous than his Hungarian contemporaries—László Moholy-

---

1 This text emerged out of the exhibition *Le Supermarché des images*, which the Jeu de Paume museum invited me to curate from February to June of 2020. I have benefited from discussions with Emmanuel Alloa and Marta Ponsa, who accompanied me on this adventure. A preliminary sketch can be found in my introductory essay to the catalogue, "Shadow Iconomics and Road Networks of the Visible," trans. Jeremy Harrison, in Peter Szendy, Emmanuel Alloa, and Marta Ponsa, eds., *The Supermarket of Images* (Paris: Gallimard / Jeu de Paume, 2020), and in my contribution to the colloquium "Vers une écologie des images," which marked the exhibition's close. A prior version of the interlude devoted to "the accident of slow motion" was written for Jean Christophe Bailly's seminar at the Jeu de Paume, the sessions of which have been subsequently collected in Bailly, ed., *Voir le temps venir* (Paris: Bayard, 2021).

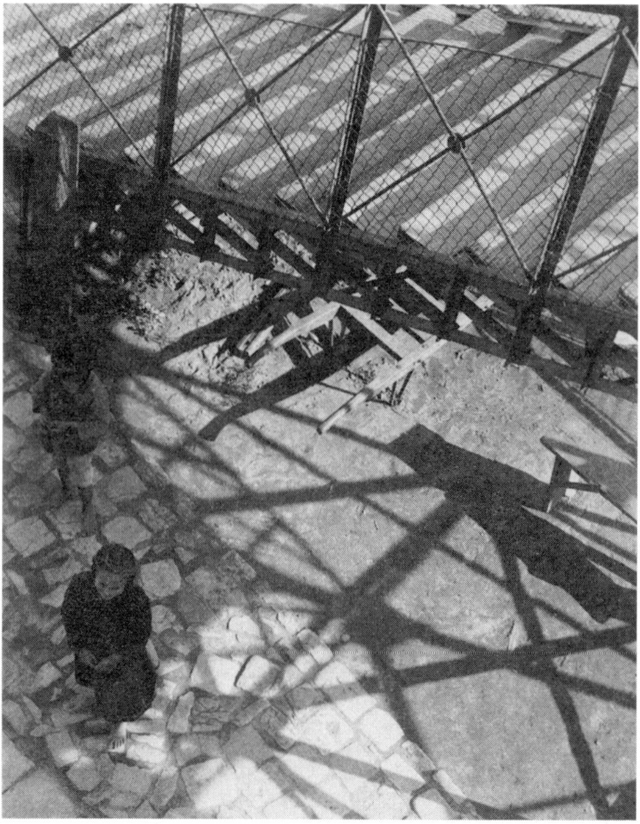

Imre Kinszki, untitled, ca. 1930s.
Courtesy of Judit Kinszki.

Nagy, Éva Besnyö, Martin Munkácsi, or Brassaï—although he was in touch with all of them. His photographs were published alongside theirs in an important 1939 anthology devoted to Hungarian photography.[2] Among these snapshots, often remarkable for their use of shadows with interwoven patterns, that of his sleeping daughter Judit is particularly close to my heart; there are uncanny views of Budapest from the 1920s and 1930s alongside images (some of them destined for scientific journals) in which the filigree of insect wings seem to echo the striations of wires and grids that crisscross cities. Imre had commissioned the firm Hock & Kiss to build a camera specially made for macro photography, christened "Kinsecta." And I can't help hearing the compounding of Kinszki and the Latin *insecta*, as if his passions for entomology and photography had crystallized in the form of this invention.

My mind wanders often to Imre bácsi, to his daughter Judit (with whom I still correspond), to my grandmother Kató who admired her brother so much, to those lives broken by deportation and the camps (Imre was seen for the last time during a death march near Sachsenhausen at the beginning of 1945; his son Gábor froze to death at Buchenwald, while Kató returned miraculously from Ravensbrück). I think of them often, but I never expected, during the research I began in order to explore the idea of an ecology of images, to discover a fascinating article by this great-uncle I had never met.

Born in 1901, Imre Kinszki had to forego his studies in biology because of a numerus clausus, or quota system, which, from 1920 onwards, limited the number of Jewish students permitted to enroll in Hungarian

2 *Magyar fényképezés* (Budapest: Officina nyomda és kiadóvállalat, 1939).

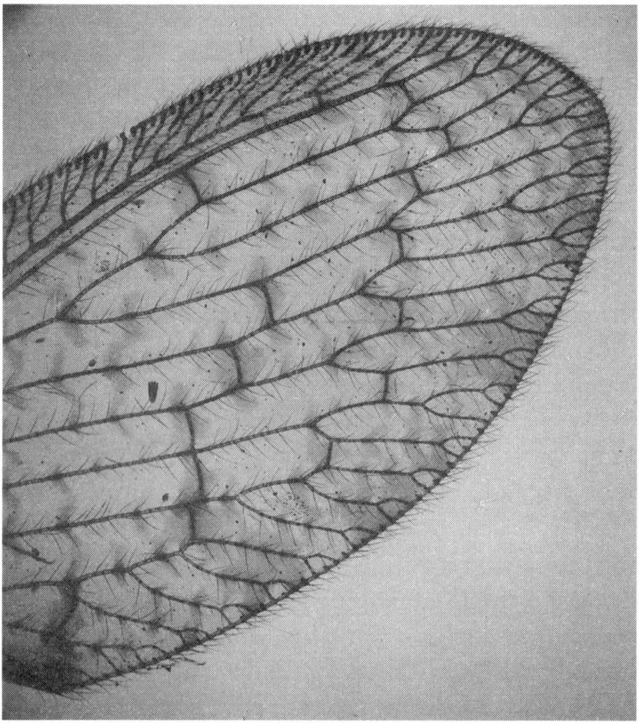

Imre Kinszki, Wing of a Lacewing, *1930s.*
Courtesy of Judit Kinszki.

universities. But this setback did not prevent him from devoting several articles to that science and its operative assumptions. Among these are the pages published in 1919 in the important journal of sociology *Huszadik század* (Twentieth century), under the following title: "A természet háztartása."[3] This simple Hungarian expression is difficult to translate: it means something like "the economy of nature," but only if you can hear the resonance with the Greek *oikonomia*, which means the keeping and running of a house or home (*oikos*). Literally, *háztartás* means "housekeeping." In lieu of a translation, I'll attempt a gloss of Imre's title: its subject is tending or attending to the house of nature.

Imre was nineteen years old when he published these pages on the economy of nature (preceded, in the same issue of the journal, by his lengthy scholarly study titled "Szükséglet, alkalmazkodás, fejlődés" [Necessity, adaptation, evolution]). He suggests that the very idea of a domestic economy on the scale of the natural world implies that nature tends toward a goal (there's no economics without a teleology, he says, without the search for a utility that cannot be measured except in relation to some desirable end). But, rather than conclude that the concept of economy was simply obsolete or worthless when applied to nature (for according to modern science, nature cannot have any goals), Imre instead adopts a "point of view" that he qualifies as "psychological." In a way that strikes me as practically Nietzschean, he turns toward "an inquiry into the genealogy of this idea, into the probable sources of its development."[4] He's not content to declare it erroneous or outmoded;

---

3 Imre Kinszki, "A természet háztartása," *Huszadik század* 20:1–2 (1919), pp. 56–8.

4 Ibid., p. 57.

he asks where it came from, why it appeared, and whose interest it serves.

All this can be summarized in a word: anthropocentrism. This is how Imre envisages what resonates for us—a century later, reading these reflections in the context of a foretold climate catastrophe—in even more urgent and dramatic fashion, that is to say the "considerable" effects that might be caused by the "thinning out or even extinction of animal and vegetable species."[5] Indeed, he says, to evaluate the consequences of the death of a living being clearly requires an "anthropocentric foundation," since "*the 'value' of the living being in question*, which is determined by its 'role' in the 'economy of nature,' means simply *the degree to which its survival is desirable for humankind*." Put another way, behind the will to protect nature and to preserve its riches is hidden, in thinly veiled form, the economic interests of humankind.

All of this leads me to believe that Imre had been reading certain writings by Ernst Haeckel, to whom we owe the word "ecology," defined in 1866 as "the science of the economy of organisms, their way of life and their vital external relationships with each other."[6] When Haeckel took it up under this new name (*Oecologie*), the idea of an economy of organic life—or the domestic

5 Ibid., p. 58.

6 Ernst Haeckel, *Generelle Morphologie der Organismen: Allgemeine Grundzüge der organischen Formen-Wissenschaft, mechanisch begründet durch die von Charles Darwin reformirte Descendenz-Theorie*, vol. 1 (Berlin: Georg Reimer, 1866), p. 8. In the aforementioned article "Szükséglet, alkalmazkodás, fejlődés," Imre Kinszki mentions Haeckel's work *Gott-Natur (Theophysis): Studien über monistische Religion* (Leipzig: Albert Kröner Verlag, 1914). [Translator's note: Unless otherwise indicated, all translations are mine.]

management of nature's house—already had a long tradition behind it. The expression "animal economy" can be found in seventeenth-century medical treatises. And the English naturalist John Ray, in his 1691 treatise *The Wisdom of God as Manifested in the Works of the Creation*, speaks of an "Oeconomy of the Plant."[7] In the following century, in 1749, Linnaeus gave the title "Oeconomia Naturae" to a dissertation that he'd authored but that, following the custom of that period, was defended by the student to whom he'd dictated it (Isaac Biberg). The first sentence reads: "By the Economy of Nature we understand the very wise disposition of natural beings instituted by the supreme creator, according to which these are suited to common ends and mutual benefit."[8]

My great-uncle Imre thus had every reason to suspect that the very idea of an economy of nature could only inherit—more or less unconsciously—these "theistic elements" bequeathed by tradition and simply carried up "beneath the wings of the drive to objectivity" that supposedly characterized modern science. More precisely,

7 John Ray, *The Wisdom of God Manifested in the Works of the Creation* (London: Samuel Smith, 1691), p. 76. The naturalist Walter Charleton also speaks about an "economy of the human body" (*Humani Corporis Oeconomia*) in his work *Oeconomia animalis novis in medicina hypothesibus superstructa et mechanice explicata* (London: Roger Daniel & John Redmayne, 1659) (literally: "a new animal economy based on medical hypotheses and explained mechanically").

8 Carolus von Linnaeus, *Oeconomia Naturae* (Uppsala, 1749). For a critique of the domestic paradigm within the idea of an economy of nature and its expansion into ecology, see Emanuele Coccia's lovely book *Metamorphoses*, trans. Robin Mackay (London: Polity, 2021), notably the chapter amusingly titled "Everybody in the House."

Imre considered that what had been "smuggled" into scientific objectivity was this doctrine of ends that animated the theological vision of nature as a household to be stewarded. And once it's a question of serving an end or a goal, Imre writes, that "can only be humankind."[9]

I'm dwelling here on these questions my great-uncle the photographer and naturalist asked back in the Hungary of 1919 because they guide me a century later, in the shadowy light of the Anthropocene, along the path I'd like to clear toward an ecology of images. In a sense, his investigations opened the way for me, even if Imre bácsi would have been unable to believe his eyes. When he left home, Kinsecta in hand, to harvest some naturalist snapshots, he could never have imagined that one day we would be uploading and circulating tens of millions of photos per hour over so-called social networks. Never could he have imagined that this tsunami of images would contribute daily—on account of the energy and raw materials required for their storage and maintenance—to "the thinning out or extinction of animal and plant species," as he called it in his article for *Huszadik század*. Yet he's the one who put me on the trail of what it means to speak about an ecology of images—not just through his vigilance with respect to anthropocentrism and teleology, but also and especially through the endlessly varied writing of shadows that his photography work offers.

Distrust of an anthropocentric teleology is more necessary than ever. Especially since images, in the age of their global circulation, belong to a regime of existence that often leads us—for what I would describe as "good bad reasons"—to want to reaffirm ourselves as the center and the sun of their iconosphere. Because these

9 Kinszki, "A természet háztartása," p. 58.

images overwhelm us from all sides, it's tempting to imagine that we could and that we must take control of them, reclaim possession of them, and, above all, guarantee a fair measure and quantity of them. That's where anthropocentrism lurks.

But what about shadows? How might an art of tracing shadows, such as Imre pursued at the moment he clicked the shutter, guide us toward the horizon of an ecology of images?

That's what I will attempt to show in the first of these two collected essays. To jump ahead for a moment: ecology, as I understand it, is not—or not only—a way of thinking about the *oikos* written into its name, that is to say about the house and the household, the concept that Imre criticized when it was applied to nature. Ecology—as I invoke it—will be the watchword for a new attention to time, to all the divergent and dissonant temporalities that work within, through, and around images. The image should be thought of as composed of these temporal layers and strata of radically heterogenous time periods, between long durations—those deep times of planetary history and evolution—and the hyper-short times of a globalized *iconomy* that disrupts the balance between them.[10] The image is, let's say, essentially *heterochronic*. And shadow, as we shall see, is one of the crucial figures through which this heterochronicity can be read and expressed.

Imre, who had daily experience of these contrasting temporalities that the nature photographer puts into play, must have known about this, I tell myself, even if

---

10 I proposed this term and an "iconomic" approach to the production and circulation of images in *The Supermarket of the Visible: Toward a General Economy of Images*, trans. Jan Plug (New York: Fordham University Press, 2019).

it was only a dim foreknowledge: the slowness of his own approach amid the swift gestures of his subjects; the tens or hundreds of millions of years it must have taken in order to produce that outline drawn by the filigreed network of an insect's wing, while the particular insect captured by the Kinsecta had the lifespan of perhaps a single day, ephemeral like the shadow cast by an oblique light that you have to wait hours for to catch at the right moment.

My ecological approach to images aims to make visible the amplitude and density of these tensions or temporal tonalities in the midst of the billions of snapshots that our social networks ferry every minute, within milliseconds, from one end of the world to the other, where they vanish almost as soon as they appear, swallowed in the flux. An ecology of images worthy of the name will bring about a resurgence of these multiple and highly contrasting durations, which the globalized circulation of images both assumes and incessantly conceals.[11] It will teach us how to see these images again—and, perhaps, to listen to them.

We will try to conceptualize the image in terms of the tension between the unspeakable slowness of its gestation according to the rhythms of the earth and the speed that, faster than light itself, carries it beyond the visible realm.

---

11 A different path toward an ecology of images would consist in putting the emphasis on their waste matter, as my friend Hervé Aubron proposes when he asks, "What does art make of discards and excreta, those of the world and those of its own making?" Hervé Aubron, "De la merde," interview by Gabriel Bortzmeyer, *Débordements*, September 10, 2015, debordements.fr.

I

Toward an Iconomy of the Nonhuman

Let us imagine, as Pliny proposes in his *Natural History*, that the first painted image was the outline of a shadow.[1] We don't know much about the beginnings of painting, but the ancient naturalist reports that, here or there, someone says that painting "began with tracing an outline round a man's shadow." We're not told much more than that, initially. But a little further along in the same volume of his monumental encyclopedia, Pliny adds a few details that have served as the basis for much commentary: he tells of the daughter of a potter of Sicyon, Butades by name. Smitten by a young man preparing to depart, she "drew in outline on the wall the shadow of his face thrown by a lamp" (umbram ex facie eius ad lucernam in pariete lineis circumscripsit).

This supposed origin of the painted image is generally evoked in order to establish that "love was the inventor of drawing" (in Rousseau's words, at the beginning of his *Essay on the Origin of Languages*). From the seventeenth century on, engravers and painters (Charles Le Brun seems to have been among the first) sought to represent the scene of the potter's daughter and her lover, as

1 Pliny, *Natural History*, vol. 9, trans. H. Rackham (Cambridge, MA: Harvard University Press, 1961), 271 and 373 (book XXXV, 5 and 43).

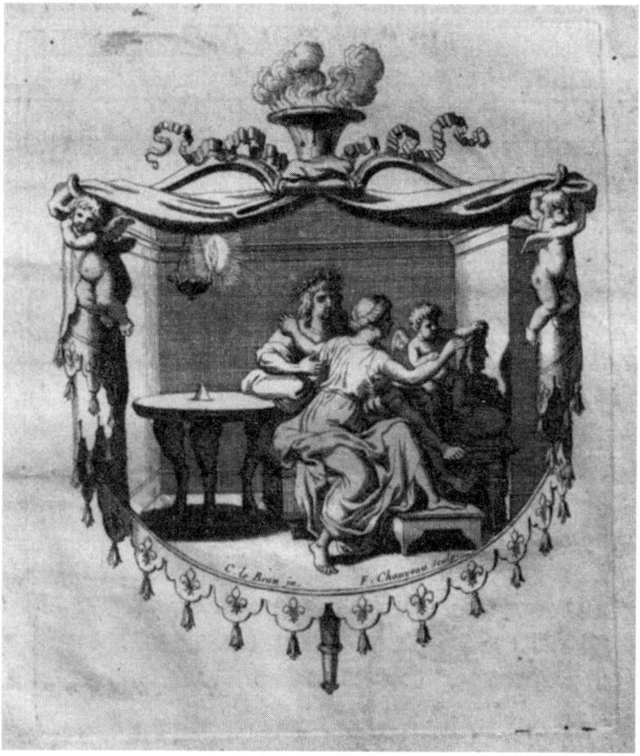

Charles Le Brun, Dibutade, *engraving (in Charles Perrault,* La Peinture *[Paris: Frederic Leonard, 1668]).*

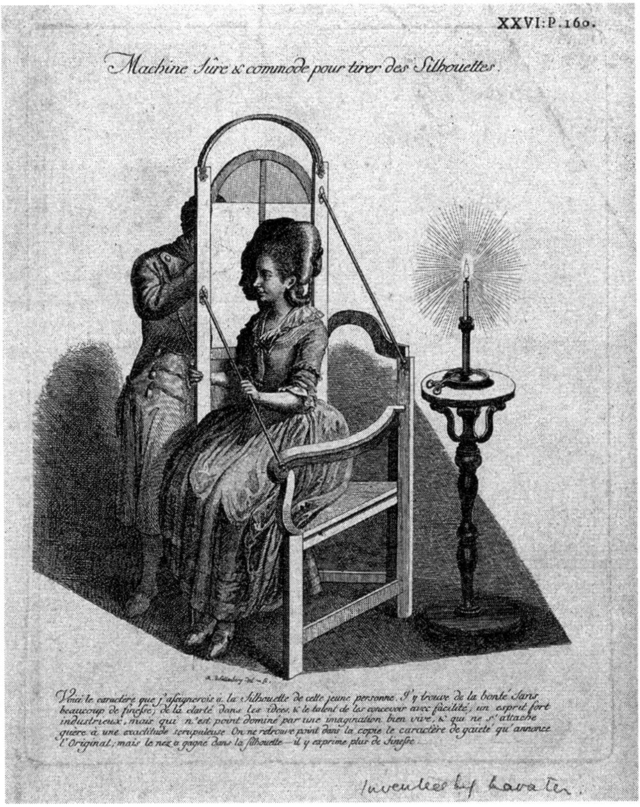

Johann Rudolph Schellenberg, Machine for Drawing Silhouettes, *engraving (in Johann Caspar Lavater,* Essai sur la physiognomonie, *vol. 2 [The Hague: Jacques van Karnebeek, 1783]).*

if painting was trying to peek into the legendary cradle of its own birth.

In the following century, this gesture of tracing a projected shadow started to become the object of serial reproductions: machines were made to realize silhouettes on the model of the "physionotrace" invented by Gilles-Louis Chrétien in 1783. The ancient shadow became henceforth an industry, mechanized and formatted to be mass produced in order to respond to a growing fashion.[2]

Often forgotten, however, in this enthusiasm for shadow drawings is what Pliny writes immediately after evoking the gesture of the potter's daughter: her father, noting what she'd done, "pressed clay" on the features she'd traced and "made a relief, which he hardened by exposure to fire with the rest of his pottery." The pictorial gesture is immediately translated into a different medium: the drawing becomes a relief in clay.

To follow Pliny's story about the birth of painting without interrupting it prematurely, it then becomes necessary to say that at the origin of the painted image, there is also its immediate reformatting (since it's a matter of formats, as we'll see) into another version, in a different edition. Or even better: at the origin of

---

2 On Gilles-Louis Chretien's "physionotrace," see René Hennequin, *Un "Photographe" de l'époque de la révolution et de l'empire: Edme Quenedey des Riceys (Aube), Portraitiste au physionotrace* (Troyes: Imprimerie de J-L Paton, 1926). The Swiss engraver Johann Rudolph Schellenberg reproduced "a comfortable and reliable machine for making silhouettes" in successive editions of Lavater's treatise on physiognomy: Johann Kaspar Lavater, *Essai sur la physiognomonie, destiné à faire connoître l'homme & à la faire aimer*, vol. 2 (The Hague: Jacques van Karnebeek, 1783), p. 160.

painting, there's an exchange, a substitution of media or of formats (from sketch to terra cotta). In the beginning, there is a difference of formatting [*formatage*], which is to say also a difference in speed, since one format (firing pottery) takes more time than the other (drawing lines). The first image in the history of art is a *transformat*.

Chasing Shadows

Pliny's fable was taken up by poets who in turn inspired the engravers illustrating their words. There is something strange about some of these representations, like the one signed by Charles-Nicolas Cochin, ornamenting a peculiar sentence taken from a poem by Antoine-Marin Le Mierre, *Painting* (1769). The verse enjoins: "Draw in your mind, it's the first canvas." In the illustration, it's almost unsettling how the shadow on the wall enlarges the profile of the beloved as if readying itself to take on a life of its own, detached from the model. (To say nothing of the father who, as if stupefied, waits while clutching the instruments of a sculptor, no longer a potter).

But it's with *Peter Schlemihl*, the extraordinary tale by Adelbert von Chamisso published in 1814, that the fantastical dimension of transformatting latent in Pliny's version really comes to light. What befalls the protagonist of this strange story? Peter Schlemihl makes a pact with a thin, pale man clothed in a gray coat—a sort of Faustian bargain: "I extended him eagerly my hand. 'Agreed! The business is done; for the purse you have my shadow!' He closed with me; kneeled instantly down before me, and I beheld him with an admirable dexterity gently loosen my shadow from top to toe from

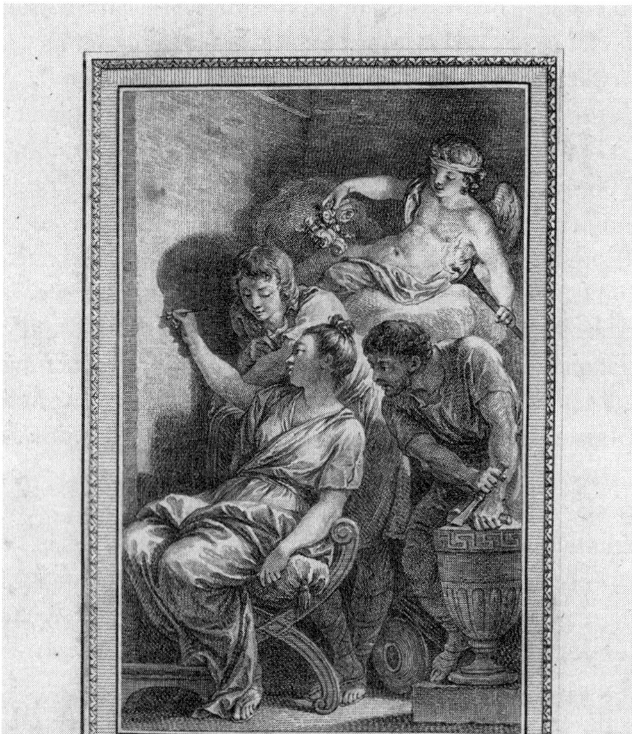

Charles-Nicolas Cochin, Dibutade, *engraving (in Antoine-Marin Le Mierre*, La Peinture *[Paris: Le Jay, 1769])*.

the grass, lift it up, roll it together, fold it, and finally pocket it."[3]

Once the pact has been sealed like this, both shadow and coins pocketed, we witness in the third chapter what looks like a fantastic reprise of the Pliny story. Now Schlemihl searches desperately to remake the shadow he has sold and seeks out "the most celebrated painter in the city." "'Mr Professor,' said I, 'could not you, think you, paint a false shadow for one who, by the most unlucky chance in the world, has become deprived of his own?'" The artist, surprised, asks in turn "through what awkwardness, through what negligence could he then lose his shadow?" Peter Schlemihl, profoundly ashamed of the bargain he struck and speaking about himself as if he were someone else responds with a lie: "In Russia, whither he made a journey last winter, in an extraordinary cold his shadow froze so fast to the ground that he could by no means loose it again." The shadow, he says in short, coagulated, crystallized, froze like ice; that is, it materialized. And once it had detached itself from the body of which it was the silhouette, it seemed impossible to reattach. "'The false shadow that I could paint him,' replied the professor, 'would only be such a one as by the slightest agitation he might lose again, especially a person who, by your relation, has so little adhesion to his own native shadow.'"

So what then becomes of the shadow in this belated and outlandish rewrite of the Plinian scene of the potter and his daughter? Perhaps we're permitted to imagine that what was implicit in Pliny's story—the transformatting and solidification of the shadow (from drawn lines

3 Adelbert von Chamisso, *The Wonderful History of Peter Schlemihl: The Man Who Lost His Shadow*, trans. Frederic Henry Hedge (Boston: Ginn & Company, 1899).

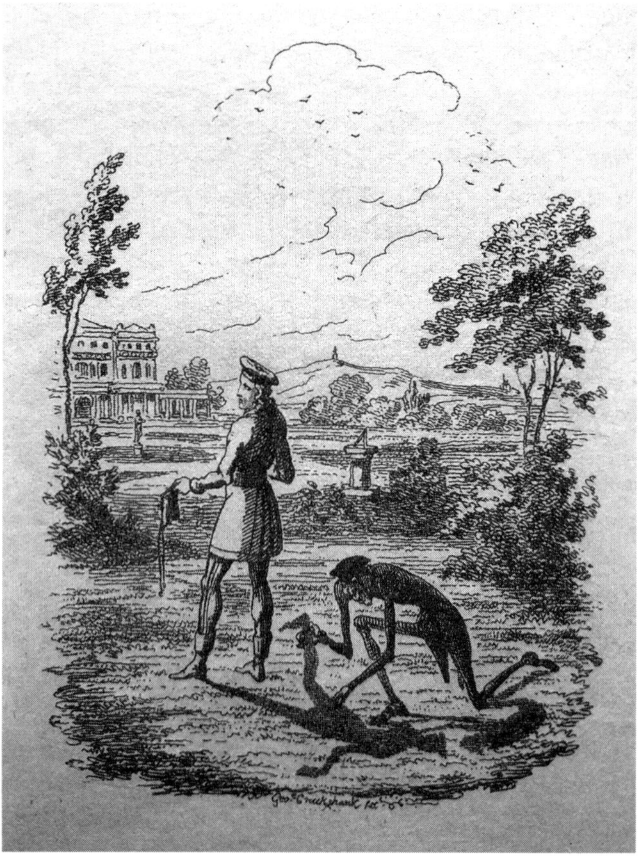

George Cruikshank, engraving (in Adelbert von Chamisso, Peter Schlemihl *[London: G & W. B. Whittaker, 1824]).*

to baked clay)—becomes explicit in Chamisso's, where the shadow, as we've just read, hardens and thickens, remaining stuck to the surface where it was projected. But the passage from one format to another (from ethereal or liquid to solid) is not only made explicit and thematized as such; it's also generalized, since it operates in two directions. In other episodes of Peter Schlemihl's fantastical tale, we see how the shadow once again loses its substance, tends toward the immaterial, and returns to a volatility that makes it seem destined to evade any efforts at capture.

This is what happens when Peter Schlemihl hurtles off in pursuit of a shadow that he hopes to appropriate: "In the sunny sand there glided past me a human shadow, not unlike my own, which, wandering there alone, seemed to have got away from its possessor ... I sprang forward to seize it. I thought that if I succeeded in treading on it so that its feet touched mine, it probably would remain hanging there and in time accommodate itself to me." The shadow flees, and Peter Schlemihl pursues —a bit like how when I was a child, my cat and I used to stalk and pounce on our own shadows—but here this chasing game, seemingly endless, comes to an abrupt halt with the most unexpected rematerialization. "I shot with a mighty spring forward to make seizure of it, and dashed unexpectedly against a hard object," the protagonist reports. The shadow in question, we learn, belongs to an invisible man, but certainly a tangible one.

What further thoughts does this fantastical story that leads us from one surprise to another have in store? If the drawing of a shadow in Pliny goes hand in hand with its transformatting into clay sculpture, the two formats nevertheless appear in succession according to a clear, defined, and directed order. This is so much the case that the second of the two formats, the modeling in clay, could just as well pass for a derivation of the first, an optional and secondary version that might easily be forgotten (in fact, as we've seen, it's more or less relegated to the margins or left out in the majority of renderings of the ancient legend, which emphasize the initial tracing of the outline). But in Chamisso's rewriting, the shadow's transformatting is so extensive that it materializes and evaporates at practically the same time: it gets detached in order to live out its own life, becoming autonomous from the body that once projected it—as if it had gained a consistency of its own, yet it flees, ungraspable; and when seemingly it must steal away to avoid being pinned down, it unexpectedly turns out to be as much the extension of a material body as ever, despite being invisible. In Chamisso, everything happens as if these multiple states and properties of the shadow coexist, as if they all define—together and simultaneously—the regime of the image's existence.

As mentioned above, the Plinian tale of the birth of painting intrigued painters and engravers like Charles Le Brun and Charles-Nicolas Cochin, who doubtless saw it as an opportunity to make an image of the process of becoming image—a meta-image of some kind. But what of Chamisso's story?

The scene of shadow hunting that we just read has been arrestingly depicted by the English illustrator George Cruikshank in an engraving made for the first English translation of *Peter Schlemihl*, published in 1824.[4] We see, of course, Schlemihl running after a

4 Adelbert von Chamisso, *Peter Schlemihl: From the German of Lamotte Fouqué* (London: G. & W. B. Whitaker, 1824). In the original German edition of 1814, the German Romantic

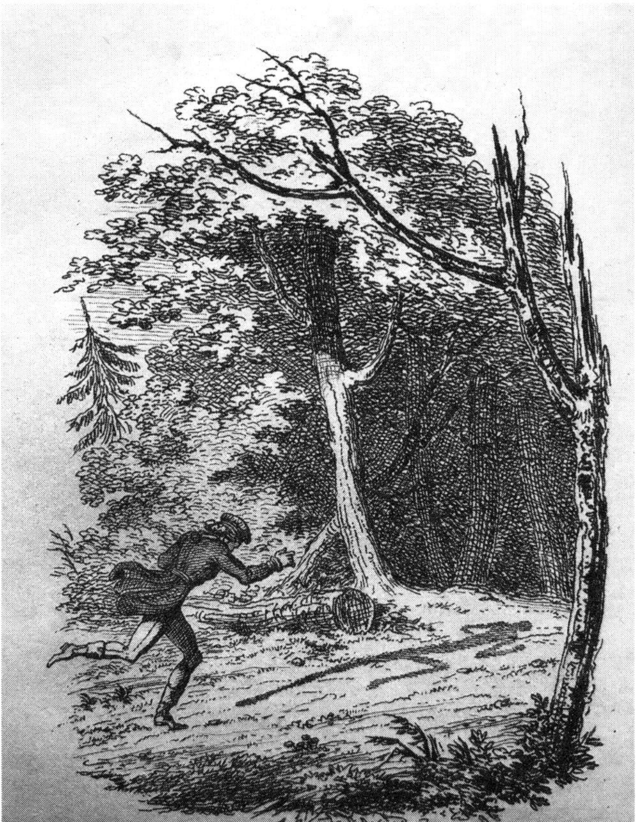

George Cruikshank, engraving (in Adelbert von Chamisso, Peter Schlemihl *[London: G & W. B. Whittaker, 1824]).*

shadow that he wishes were his own, that is to say his self-image. Peter Schlemihl is running after his own image. But if we think about this illustration, in the light of Charles Le Brun and Charles-Nicolas Cochin, as a meta-image, as an image of the coming-into-being of images, then we'd be better off describing it this way: what we're seeing is an image (of Peter Schlemihl) chasing after an image of itself (his shadow).

The image running after its own image. There it is, the most fantastic mise-en-scène of the temporal disjunction that is perhaps at work in every image. The image here is literally ahead of (or behind) itself.

Cruikshank (who also illustrated Dickens and *Tristram Shandy*) thus allows us to think about the image as a frozen differential of speeds, provisionally stabilized and held in suspense. That differential, as we've seen, is already implicitly at work in the original Pliny story about the invention of painting, between drawing and casting with clay. It is even more explicit in Chamisso's retelling—and yet more so in those images of today's digital age that traverse our so-called social networks, millions of them transported each minute by undersea cables or by radioelectric waves relayed by satellites orbiting the planet.[5]

---

writer Friedrich de la Motte-Fouqué, Chamisso's friend, was named as the manuscript's "editor."

5 I will return to the history of the orbital transformation of road networks of the visible in the chapter devoted to "Iconomy on a Universal Scale." The history of cables deserves an entire study of its own. This would draw upon the pioneering work of Nicole Starosielski, *The Undersea Network* (Durham, NC: Duke University Press, 2015), and Keller Easterling, "Broadband," in *Extrastatecraft: The Power of Infrastructure Space* (London: Verso, 2014). The "new geography of cables" through

The story of Peter Schlemihl comes only a few decades before the appearance of the first trans-Atlantic telecommunication cable, thanks to which, in 1858, a telegram was sent at a speed of about two minutes per letter. The guy who sold his shadow to the diabolical man in gray was already moving faster than that. When he's lucky enough to find a pair of "seven-leagued boots," he begins to roam the length, width, and breadth of the planet at a speed that keeps pace even with those breathlessly circulating images of our contemporary iconomic space: "I passed at the pillars of Hercules over to Europe, and when I had reviewed the southern and northern provinces I crossed from northern Asia over the polar glaciers to Greenland and America." Globe-trotting in all directions, the journeys of Peter Schlemihl accelerate to the point of madness through a kind of frenetic oscillation that makes him flee "the excessive cold" of the Norwegian coastline for the burning rays of the Libyan deserts and then back again: "I ran with swift, uncertain steps, from west to east, from east to west. I found myself now in the day, now in the night; now in

---

which today's internet passes, Starosielski suggests, is superposed upon "a geopolitical matrix of preexisting colonial and national routes." Rithy Panh's documentary *The Land of Wandering Souls* (2000) offers another astonishing example. In 1999, the director followed the laying of the first fiber-optic cable to traverse Cambodia, on behalf of the French telecom company Alcatel. The cable linked Southeast Asia to China and thence to Europe. Wielding pickaxes barefooted, the workers were paid poverty wages (the equivalent of sixty cents per meter dug), and their families were often reduced to begging for food. This is how "an information superhighway" is made, a highway that "followed the old silk road through Cambodia." Rithy Panh, "La parole filmée: Pour vaincre la terreur," *Communications* 71 (2001), p. 377.

summer, now in the winter's cold." It is almost as if—as he passes from hot to cold as something passes from liquid to solid or invisible to visible—the man with a shadow that's sometimes stable and sometimes volatile also begins to exist, like the images that surround us, in a regime of perpetual transformatting.

On Transimages without Humans

How do they actually circulate, these digital images of which the tale of Peter Schlemihl is a kind of anticipatory allegory? They form—or coagulate (they crystallize, one might say, echoing the frozen shadow from Chamisso's story)—as a result of hidden and practically instantaneous operations of coding and formatting. This secret writing through which contemporary images become visible (what I've elsewhere referred to as their "steganography") determines in particular their weight: each image materializes (or freezes) in a whole series of formats (JPEG, PNG, GIF, TIFF), with a rate of compression that affects the data which composes it.[6] It exists simultaneously in higher or lower resolutions, that is, in lighter or heavier versions of itself. These different weights and sizes will determine the image's tendency to circulate, as well as its capacity for diffusion and the speed it can travel (a high-definition image requires more time and consumes more energy to deliver). The digital image cannot be disassociated from its transformattings and is always ahead of or behind itself (ahead of or behind another crystallization or alternate state of itself).

6 Peter Szendy, *The Supermarket of the Visible: Toward a General Economy of Images*, trans. Jan Plug (New York: Fordham University Press, 2019), p. 114.

But we must go further: not only does the same image exist within different digital formats, but once these images are uploaded and put into circulation from one end of the world to the other, through fiberoptic cables or electromagnetic waves, they are also dissected into discrete packets of data: pieces precede other pieces of themselves down the pathways and networks that make up our contemporary infrastructure of the visible. These images in transit, or *transimages* (passing not just from one screen to another but also from one state of being into another), *are in the process of becoming the images that they are*: they condense and coagulate and take shape, but they are also always unmaking themselves; they are disassembled and distributed in segments that can reform as they were or be rearranged otherwise.

But let us pause for a second to catch our breath. Why have we followed Peter Schlemihl into this frantic race? And where are we in its course?

From the Plinian fable about the origins of painting to today's digital images, the image is a transformat that is both behind and also ahead of itself. But as vast and even as vertiginous as our historical scope might feel, running as it does from Pliny to the worldwide web, can we really affirm so matter-of-factly that *every* image is but a temporarily stabilized differential of speeds? After all, the images that we've considered so far are all, in one way or another, attached to the human—both to the human figure and to human means of production. Even a shadow detached from the body that projected it remains a kind of human excrescence (like nails or hair or an animal's feathers, with which Gilbert Simondon compares the image in a text we'll soon come to).[7]

---

7 "Hair and fingernails have the virtue of extremities: they express the insertion of the body in the outside world,

The images with which we've so far been dealing are hardly representative of everything that might be subsumed under the category of image. Pliny, in the last two books of his *Natural History* dedicated to mineralogy, mentions other images that humankind played no role in producing. On the subject of the white Parian marble, he reports that "when the stone-breakers split a single block with their wedges, a likeness of Silenus was found inside." Later on, he speaks of a precious stone belonging to Pyrhhus, "an agate on which could be seen the Nine Muses with Apollo holding his lyre. This was due not to any artistic intention, but to nature unaided." He adds, "The markings spread in such a way that even the individual Muses had their appropriate emblems allotted to them."[8] These ancient images born out of pure chance deserve to be called *acheiropoiēta*, a term we also find in Paul (2 Corinthians 5:1) to designate the celestial realm, "the eternal abode that was not made by the hand of man." The word (from the

---

materializing and expressing its limits, its active borders; anything that is mobile and visible is already virtually detachable from the individual in order to keep on expressing his force and possibilities of action; that which is sufficiently pliable and mobile in the body to serve expression, such as hair and the extremities of limbs, tends to be selected as an intermediary object preserving absolute properties; the symbolic function is continuous with the skin appendages of various species, since these appendages manifest a relational category of the organism, existing for and towards the outside as organs of display [*manifestation*]." Gilbert Simondon, *Imagination and Invention*, trans. Joe Hughes and Christophe Wall-Romana (Minneapolis: University of Minnesota Press, 2022), pp. 133–4.

8 Pliny, *Natural History*, vol. 10, trans. D. E. Eichholz (Cambridge, MA: Harvard University Press, 1971), 13 (book XXXVI, 4) and 167 (book XXXVII, 3).

Greek for hand, *kheir*) was later employed to describe those images made by the miracle of pure divine grace, without human intervention.

It appears the first use of the term in its iconological meaning can be found in a Syriac chronicle from around 569 CE, probably put together by a monk known by the name of "Pseudo-Zacharias," since he also incorporated the *Ecclesiastical History* of Zacharias Rhetor. Book XII of the chronicle records that one day in the Cappadocian village of Camulia, a woman named Hypatia discovered the image of Christ painted on a scrap of linen floating in a well in her garden. When she pulled it from the water, the image wasn't even wet. Hypatia covered it with a veil and brought it to the preceptor who was preparing her to convert to the Christian faith. In transit, the image produced a copy of itself onto Hypatia's veil. Later, another woman, unnamed in the chronicle, brings back a second copy of the image found in the well to her house near Amasea, in the north of contemporary Turkey. The chronicle notes that in this region the image (*eikōn*) is called *akheiropoiētos*, "which means 'not made by hands.'"[9]

Whether in veins of stone or a portrait of Christ, the acheiropoetic image is whatever fashions *itself* without human aid. But in the case of the image Hypatia finds at Camulia, the image's reproduction also bypasses

9 The text of the Syriac chronicle appears in a recent English translation as *The Chronicle of Pseudo-Zachariah Rhetor*, trans. Robert R. Phenix and Cornela B. Horn (Liverpool: Liverpool University Press, 2011); see also Ernst Kitzinger's study "The Cult of Images in the Age Before Iconoclasm," *Dumbarton Oaks Papers* 8 (1954), which identifies the chronicle as the earliest known appearance of the term *akheiropoiētos* applied to an image.

any manufacture, handling, or maintenance. The image *self*-duplicates over the course of its transportation from where it was first seen. Essentially transferable, it declares its independence not only from the medium where it was found (it was not dampened by the well water where it floated) but also from the surfaces where it momentarily appears (the scrap of linen and the veil), as if these were photographic prints. It is unsurprising, then, that photography should conjure the imaginary, and even the lexicon, of Christian acheiropoetics while explicitly inscribing itself from its beginnings into a history of the material-immaterial tracing of shadows.[10]

10 In his account of "photogenic drawing" obtained "without aid of the artist's pencil" (i.e., placing the object directly on a sheet of photosensitive paper), Henry Fox Talbot devotes a brief but fascinating section to "the art of fixing a shadow" or "the most transitory of things" (*Some Account of the Art of Photogenic Drawing, or The Process by Which Natural Objects May Be Made to Delineate Themselves Without the Aid of the Artist's Pencil* [London: R. & J. E. Taylor, 1839], pp. 6–7). Taking up a word that already appears in both Plato and Aristotle, Talbot designates images obtained in this fashion as "Sciagraphy," that is, shadow writing (he speaks of the "sciagraphic process" in his notebooks); see Larry Schaaf, *Records of the Dawn of Photography, Talbot's Notebooks P&Q* (Cambridge: Cambridge University Press, 1996), p. xviii. In 1857, the Swedish photographer Gustav Rejlander produced a parody of the Plinian scene: *The First Negative* is a photograph of the British actor John Coleman sitting while a young woman (seen from behind) traces the outline of his shadow on the wall. In *Camera Lucida*, Barthes wonders "might we not say of it [photography] what the Byzantines said of the image of Christ which impregnated St. Veronica's napkin: that it was not made by the hand of man, *acheiropoiētos?*" Roland Barthes, *Camera Lucida: Reflections on Photography*, trans. Richard Howard (New York: Hill & Wang, 1981), p. 82. Even as photography

Acheiropoetic: this is what contemporary photography has mostly become, as a majority of its uses short-circuit not only the human hand but also the retinal destination of the image. For neither fingers nor eyes are involved in the decoding of a snapshot taken by the automatic cameras used to read license plates, the kind we encounter everywhere on highways, at toll stations, or mounted on police cars. Neither hands nor pupils intervene in the recording, circulation, and analysis of these type of surveillance images in general (whether they originate in shopping centers, airports, train stations, metro stations, residential lobbies, banks, or cash machines), just as they play no part in the robotic management of stocks and deliveries thanks to electronic recognition of packages and bar codes. As the American artist Trevor Paglen writes, "the overwhelming majority of images" are now produced "by machines for other machines with humans rarely in the loop." This ever-growing part of the visible world actually escapes the sensory-motor grasp of humans and constitutes an "invisible visual culture."[11]

---

recalls the processes of acheiropoesis, the opposite is no less true: Georges Didi-Huberman speaks about "prints" [*tirage*] when describing the production and reproduction of acheiropoetic images in *La Ressemblance par contact* (Paris: Minuit 2008), p. 90. And Jean-Christophe Bailly, in his magnificent essay *The Instant and Its Shadow*, trans. Samuel E. Martin (New York: Fordham University Press, 2020), extends the notion of *acheiropoiētos* to "the photographic effects of the atomic bomb," which, for example, produced "on an electricity pole near the Meiji Bridge, the imprinted shadow of leaves."

11 Trevor Paglen, "Invisible Images (Your Pictures Are Looking at You)," *The New Inquiry*, December 8, 2016. The acheiropoiesis of contemporary images is based, however, on a labor force whose alienated acheiropoesis remains, as of this

Henceforth, since humans are an increasingly marginal factor in the genesis and becoming of images, it's clear that we cannot think about images without breaking with this centripetal motion that makes them orbit around ourselves. This is why I'm exploring here the possibility of an iconocentric ecology of images, in order to open up an *anthropofugal* exit, to sketch out that step beyond a restricted iconomy of images produced by and for humans. And the question guiding me is that of the image *in general* as a transformat, as a differential of speeds, ahead of or behind itself. Put

---

writing, less expensive than pure machine artificial intelligence; cf. Antonio Casilli, *En attendant les robots: Enquête sur le travail du clic* (Paris: Seuil, 2019). Click farms featuring hundreds of screens and thousands of SIM cards are the assembly lines of the contemporary visual sphere, as is readily apparent in Martin Le Chevallier's video installation *Clickworkers* (2017). The video gives a voice to those whose daily labor contributes to the organization and distribution of images in circulation. The same still frame of an empty room is accompanied by an offscreen feminine voice that recounts, in deliberate monotone, snippets of a fictive autobiography that is nonetheless all too real: "I am a tagger," testifies Magda from Krakow, Poland. "I tag images on my computer … I work ten, fifteen, sometimes twenty hours a day. But I don't even make a worker's salary. I look at porn, beheadings, stuff like that, and I tag them. I put labels on them. I characterise them: terrorism, violence, pedophilia. I suppose these images are later filed or censored. But I know nothing more about them. I can't know." Later the voice becomes a different woman's, Rihaa from Dhaka in Bangladesh. She speaks about the "little team" she's a part of: "Each one of us manages several hundred accounts and we like. We sell likes by the thousands. Likes by the kilo. We spend all our time liking … We also do views, views of videos by the thousands. We watch without watching. Hours, days, entire lives of videos that we pretend to have watched."

otherwise, we're wondering whether, before or beyond a human timescale, the image can still be conceived of as essentially and structurally heterochronic. Crucially, an image results from a certain tension or elasticity in time, from a "tone" (from the Greek *tonos*, used in speaking about a stretched string or of the tendon of a muscle).

Thinking the image as tensive and tensile—or thinking about the tone of images—that's what I'm putting to the test here by exploring what I'm calling "a nonhuman iconomy." But before we get there: let me take a brief detour required to understand the recent history of an idea.

The Ecology of Images: An Aborted Idea?

Can we—must we—put under the sign of an ecology of images our effort to exit the sphere of an anthropocentric iconomy? If it's the case, ever since Haeckel coined the term, that an ecology is first of all a "natural economy," don't we always risk "smuggling" (as my great-uncle Imre used to say) an anthropocentrism that we would have preferred to leave out? In speaking about an ecology of images, aren't we making a prejudicial judgment about the value that images in general have *for us*? In fact, I'm going to try to defend a different way of thinking, based on the horizon of interpretation I've opened in the course of our reading of the shadow stories of Pliny and Chamisso: the image as a heterochronicity, that is, as a differential of speeds.

But we should already be asking ourselves: When we speak about an ecology of images, when we use that phrase, what legacy comes with it? Where do these words come from? I only know of a few recent and rare occurrences of the expression, mere suggestions that do not really rise to a level that would constitute a field of inquiry in its own right. Susan Sontag was the first, to my knowledge, to advance the idea of "an ecology not only of real things but of images as well."[12] These are the last lines of her 1977 essay on photography. So we are left in suspense. From the preceding paragraphs, we can infer that an ecology of images would be called upon as an antidote to the consumerist logic of an infinite surplus of pictures ("we need still more images; and still more," Sontag writes). This antidote is said to be necessary even if images aren't threatened with extinction or exhaustion, even though—or rather precisely because—their reserves are unlimited: "Just because they are an unlimited resource, one that cannot be exhausted by consumerist waste, there is all the more reason to apply the conservationist remedy." But when Sontag returns to this same idea one year before her death and repeats the same phrase in *Regarding the Pain of Others*, when she asserts that we are "flooded" in images "that once used to shock and arouse indignation," when she laments that "compassion, stretched to its limits, is going numb," she then concludes categorically that *there will never be an ecology of images*, that no one can ration horror or "keep fresh its ability to shock."[13] In short, the very idea of conservation applied to images is without hope.

In 1992, between the belated birth of the idea of an ecology of images and its precipitous obsequies, the sociologist Andrew Ross had tried to grow the seed Sontag

12 Susan Sontag, *On Photography* (New York: Farrar, Straus & Giroux, 1977).

13 Susan Sontag, *Regarding the Pain of Others* (New York: Farrar, Straus & Giroux, 2003), p. 108.

had planted. In an essay titled, in fact, "The Ecology of Images," his attention is drawn to images of the first Gulf War, particularly to pictures of the oil spills in the Persian Gulf. These spills were strategic, an attempt by Iraqi forces to forestall an American amphibious assault. But it was also a propaganda war—a war of images—that they unleashed: in the American press, CNN leading the charge, the military and environmental threats kept getting mixed up or superimposed, the dark tides of oil often an implicit figuration of "the sinister and inexorable spread of Islam/Arab nationalism."[14]

Ross then proposes to distinguish between "images of ecology" and an "ecology of images," so as better to consider how these might interact. The former, he writes, constitute "a genre of images," comprised of well-known clichés:

> on the one hand, belching smokestacks, seabirds mired in petrochemical sludge, fish floating belly up, traffic jams in Los Angeles and Mexico City, and clear cut forests; on the other hand, the redemptive repertoire of pastoral imagery, crowned by the ultimate global spectacle, the fragile, vulnerable ball of spaceship Earth.

After having listed these "images of ecology," Ross then wonders what an ecology of images might be, "whether images have an ecology in their own right." This leads him to consider "the social and industrial organization of images," to consider how "images are produced, distributed, and used in modern electronic culture."[15]

---

14 Andrew Ross, "The Ecology of Images," in *Eloquent Obsessions: Writing Cultural Criticism*, ed. Marianna Torgovnick (Durham, NC: Duke University Press, 1994), p. 187.

15 Ibid., p. 190.

Here Ross subjects Sontag's earlier proposition to a piercing critique. By deploring the "image overload in our modern information society," by accusing the proliferation of pictures of "*depleting* reality," Sontag doesn't take into account those cases where it's precisely the images themselves that allow us to struggle against "the material disappearance of the real" and help "counteract the destruction of the natural world."[16] In other words, if Sontag's proposition is ultimately "disappointing," as Ross says, it's because she concedes too much to the commonplace of a "surfeit of information" and thus blocks the possibility that *images themselves might prove resistant to their effects*. Retrospectively, in light of more recent work, we can say that the critical debate between Ross and Sontag is about the ecology of attention.[17]

Over the course of his case for the activist power of images of ecology, Ross mentions in passing "the chemical underpinnings of the film economy." In this way, he opens up another perspective on the ecology of images: that of the direct environmental impact of their production and circulation on a large scale. A number of recent works have confirmed how much the supposedly immaterial universe of digital images formatted as JPEGs or MP4s has an alarming material, ecological, and geopolitical impact. Data centers and server farms must be air-conditioned; cables destabilize the ecosystems through which they run; recycling screens and devices leaves toxic by-products; the extraction of metals necessary for batteries diverts or contaminates

16 Ibid., p. 197.

17 See Yves Citton's remarkable synthesis devoted to this question, *The Ecology of Attention*, trans. Barnaby Norman (Cambridge: Polity Press, 2017).

freshwater supplies and destroys the ocean depths while also exacerbating the dynamics of neocolonial exploitation. If we are to develop Andrew Ross's intuition, the project of an ecology of images needs to go further than the images of black tides (like those during the Gulf War) or the unceasing luminescent tide of digital images, and take account of "deep time"—what Jussi Parikka calls a "geology" or "geophysics" of media: the contemporary iconomy would be impossible without metals and metalloids such as lithium for batteries, indium for liquid crystal screens, and germanium for fiberoptics.[18]

The Mycelium of Iconogenesis

Among these different perspectives that converge toward or diverge from the project of an ecology of images, there is one that remains relatively unexplored: the deep time and duration proper to images produced by what we might provisionally think of as "nature"—without asking too many questions about that word for the moment. Take as an example—one that my great-uncle

18 Jussi Parikka, *A Geology of Media* (Minneapolis: University of Minnesota Press, 2015), esp. p. 52, where the author takes care to distinguish his approach from that of the media archeologist Siegfried Zielinski, who also refers to "deep time" but means by that the complex protohistory of modern media such as it appears already with, for example, "medieval alchemists." For his part, Parikka makes the case for "an alternative deep time" that encompasses "a geophysics of media culture." For an overview of the ecological risks of contemporary media, see Sean Cubitt, *Finite Media: Environmental Implications of Digital Technologies* (Durham, NC: Duke University Press, 2017).

Imre might have suggested—the pattern and figures that appear on butterfly wings. The temporality in question here belongs neither to the relatively short period of manmade images—whether by hand or by analog then digital machines—nor is it part of deep mineral time, the eras of geologic accumulation of raw materials (metals and fossil fuels) necessary for the industrial and postindustrial circulation of those manmade images. The long unfolding and duration of the image that I'd like to explore in several of its aspects is more about *the natural formation of images between, among, and from themselves*. I'd like to clear a path for a general iconomy that would ultimately resonate with the governing idea of a deep ecology.[19]

In order to approach the question of long-term iconogenesis, let us first turn to the remarkable posthumous work of Gilbert Simondon, *Imagination and Invention*, a series of lecture courses he gave at the Sorbonne in 1965 and1966. Already in his "preamble," the argument is at once restrained and enlarged in accordance with a paradoxical double move that creates all the interest, contains all the tension, and constitutes the *tone* of the entire Simondonian project: "A mental image," he writes, "is a relatively independent subset within the living being qua subject [*être vivant sujet*]."[20] It is not therefore a question of images in general; the course limits itself to dealing with an enclave of images contained within a living being. But—and here's the enlargement that counterbalances the restriction—he attributes a relative independence to this enclave of images. Put another way,

19 As sketched out by Arne Naess in "The Shallow and the Deep, Long-Range Ecology Movement," *Inquiry: An Interdisciplinary Journal of Philosophy* 16, no. 1 (1973), pp. 95–100.

20 Simondon, *Imagination and Invention*, p. 3.

we can say that the realm of mental images we contain could very well overflow the container; it could reveal itself to be larger and vaster than the image repository that we ourselves are, we the living (and it's not for nothing that Simondon voluntarily leaves open the question of knowing whether this "living being" and bearer of images must be human).

And here we reach the decisive turn in Simondon's argument: this autonomous but also overflowing enclave of "the mental image" (the work of the "reproductive imagination") does not exist only as a simple collection and storehouse of accumulated images. It obeys its own cyclic rhythms, a "cycle of images" that goes through successive "phases" that constitute "a single process of genesis, comparable in its unfolding to the other genetic processes that the living world shows us (both phylogenesis and ontogenesis)."[21] What Simondon attempts to show is not only how living beings make—or allow to bloom—within themselves those images that traverse and also reciprocally form them but, above all, how these images themselves result from transformations and metamorphoses whose laws are analogues to those of the evolution of living species (phylogenesis) or of individuals (ontogenesis).

To speak of "a mental image" when referring to these mobile and cyclic pictorial formations that blossom and wither within us living beings is to use a vocabulary that may be misleading—all the more because Simondon himself notes that the "mental content of which we can be conscious" results from "cases of an almost exceptional surfacing [*affleurement*]." Then, using a mycelial metaphor, Simondon further suggests that what's of

21 Ibid., pp. 3–4.

importance to iconogenesis over the long term is less "the visible part of the mushroom"—that is, those images that emerge in conscious life—than the "infrastructure that carries them along," namely the "mycelium," that ensemble of buried filaments that, without ever appearing aboveground, nonetheless "proliferates."[22]

If the preamble to *Imagination and Invention* is placed initially under the sign of the mental image as it exists "within the living being qua subject," it nevertheless quickly becomes clear that the image in question is also, and above all, that which "refuses to let the subject's will direct it, and *presents itself according to its own forces*, living in our consciousness like an intruder disturbing the order of a household."[23] Iconogenesis obeys its own laws while *passing through the subject*, and parasitizing it.

Simondon here recalls "the most rationalist of the ancient philosophers," those who swore by the materialism of images, like Lucretius, who in his *De rerum natura* explains the formation of images from simulacra —that is, membranes or bark (*membranae vel cortex*) that detach from things. Far from sweeping this away as a curiosity of interest only to intellectual historians of antiquity, Simondon understands the Lucretian theory (which is to say the Epicurean theory) about the "physical causes" of the image as one more confirmation of its "potent exteriority and relative independence ... with respect to the subject."[24] The image's status, he says, is that of a "quasi-organism," a virus or a guest parasite, "inhabiting the subject and developing within it."

22 Ibid., p. 4.

23 Ibid., p. 7, emphasis added.

24 Ibid., pp. 8–9, translation modified.

Simondon initially multiplies analogies in his attempt to grasp this materiality and viral reproducibility of the image: it is "endowed with a ghostly power"—it "overcomes the subject," it insinuates itself "as we say a ghost can walk through walls," and it ends up "like a foreign population in the midst of an orderly state." But in order to translate the mobile density of images—since "each image has a weight, a certain force"—these comparisons to spectral forms or immigrant populations soon give way to what will remain the central and dominant paradigm of the discourse of iconogenesis: that of the living organism.[25] Simondon resorts constantly to this, in particular in the following crucial passage:

> Studies of ontogenesis have shown that growth processes do not cover the organs and functional systems of a living being in a uniform way: there are lags in each partial growth relative to the others, and there are different speeds, especially among complex organisms, so much so that it is difficult to establish the exact moment at which an organism reaches its complete adult stage; moreover, growth and development display stages and cycles, separated by periods of transition in which a dedifferentiation is followed by a reorganization ... Mental images ... would thus possess a genetic dynamism analogous to that of an organ or a system of organs on a trajectory of growth.[26]

For all intents and purposes, the image behaves like an organism, says Simondon. And this passage is crucial to what interests me here since, by proposing an analogy between ontogenesis (the development and growth of

25 Ibid., pp. 8–10.
26 Ibid., p. 18.

an individual) and what I continue to call iconogenesis (the "genetic dynamism" of images),[27] Simondon—as we've just read—emphasizes the differences in phase or the differentials of speed at work in them, images and organisms both.

Several pages earlier, Simondon provides a particularly apt turn of phrase that crystallizes this idea of the image-organism tugged between diverging temporalities over the course of its development. Borrowing the language of developmental biology, he writes that these "image-objects are quasi-organisms, or at least seeds, capable of being reborn and developing in the subject." And, he adds, "even outside of the subject, they multiply … propagating and reproducing themselves in a *neotenic state* until they find the opportunity to become reabsorbed and redeployed in *the imaginal phase*."[28]

What is this enigmatic "neotenic state" of images? And what is their "imaginal stage"?

Drawing over Millions of Years

Let's try to understand what Simondon might mean when he speaks about a neoteny of images. The word *Neotenie* was coined in 1884 by the German anatomist Julius Kollmann in order to describe those organisms which, in an adult state, "maintain their juvenile form."[29]

---

27 In his short but excellent summary, Emmanuel Alloa proposes the term "eikogenesis." Emmanuel Alloa, "Prégnances du devenir: Simondon et les images," *Critique* 816 (2015), p. 370.

28 Simondon, *Imagination and Invention*, p. 13, emphasis added, translation modified.

29 Julius Kollmann, "Das Ueberwintern von europaïschen Frosch- und Tritonlarven und die Umwandlung des mexikanischen

Kollmann explains that the word is composed of two Greek roots, *neos*—young—and *teinō*—to extend, prolong, stretch. A classic example of neoteny is the female glowworm (*Lampyris noctiluca*), which attains an adult state capable of reproduction (her light is precisely what attracts males) while also keeping traits belonging to her larval state. There's a tension between her capacity for adult reproduction and the persistence of those larval characteristics, like the absence of wings (unlike males of the same species). To speak as Simondon does of a "neotenic" state of the image is thus to suggest by analogy that there's something that stretches or pulls the image between two different states. The neotenic image would therefore be an image that's both an adult and a larva. What holds it together would be the tension of this *-tenic* stretching.

The image, to extend the metaphor of bioluminescence, is that which glows and appears out of a time difference, from what we could call—borrowing from a coinage of Ernst Haeckel's back in 1875—a *heterochronicity*. Haeckel minted this neologism in the framework of his theory of recapitulation: ontogenesis (the development of an individual), he thought, would be a condensed repetition of phylogenesis (the development of the species), albeit with certain "lags"—that is, either advances or delays in the parallelism between the two. (Over the course of its growth, the individual might develop certain characteristics earlier or later than might be expected from the order of their appearance in the history of the species.)[30] Heterochronicity is, in sum,

Axolotl," *Verhandlungen der naturforschenden Gesellschaft in Basel* 7, no. 2 (1884), p. 391.

30 Ernst Haeckel, *Anthropogenie oder Entwicklungsgeschichte des Menschen* (Leipzig: Verlag von Wilhelm Engelmann,

either an anticipatory or postponed development (eventually postponed forever, as in the case of the neoteny of female glowworms, who reproduce without ever having acquired all the traits of adults).

A particularly astonishing case of heterochronic development is provided in an 1876 study that August Weismann devoted to the genesis of the shapes and colored lines borne by various caterpillars.[31] The ontogenetic development of the caterpillar—the larva—of the elephant hawk moth (*Chaerocampa elpenor*) takes a little less than a month before it transforms into its chrysalis. Initially one notes a fine white subdorsal line curving toward the top. Afterwards, a black line underlines and encircles, little by little, these curves, eventually giving "the impression of a large eye"—what naturalists call an "ocellus"—while the white line disappears almost entirely.

Weismann's hypothesis is that some of the designs that appear on the body of this animal had in the past a protective function, either through mimicry (as in camouflage) or intimidation. The "white, longitudinal lines," for example, "heighten the protective resemblance" of the caterpillar as it melds with its environment by

---

1877), p. 11. On the complicated history of the concept of heterochronicity in evolutionary theory, see Stephen Jay Gould, *Ontogeny and Phylogeny* (Cambridge, MA: Harvard University Press, 1977), p. 82ff.

31 August Weismann, "Die Entstehung der Zeichnung bei den Schmetterlings-Raupen," in *Studien zur Descendenz-Theorie*, vol. 2 (Leipzig: Verlag von Wilhelm Engelmann, 1876), pp. 1–137. I'm citing the summarized version of this study that Weismann himself provides in *The Evolution Theory*, vol. 2, trans. J. Arthur Thomson and Margaret R. Thomson (London: Edward Arnold, 1904), pp. 177–85.

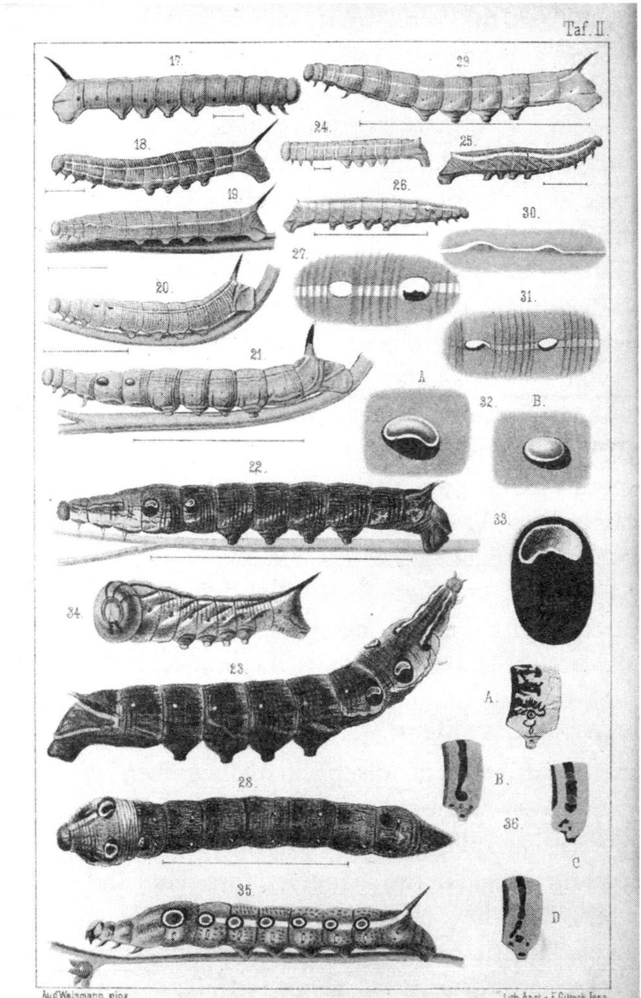

*August Weismann, eyespots and stripes in the caterpillar of the elephant hawk (*Studien zur Descendenz-Theorie*, vol. 2 [Leipzig: Verlag von Wilhelm Engelmann, 1876]).*

"mimicking the sharp light reflections on the grass-stems," and the "spots" that "imitate the eyes of a larger animal and have a terrifying effect" thereby discourage predators. These protective functions, explains Weismann, evolved over the course of history: "The ancestors of these species of *Chaerocampa* possessed longitudinal stripes in the adult state" that protected them through camouflage in the middle of meadows; but "later, when the species changed their habitat to plants with broad leaves which had arisen in the meantime, eye-spots were developed." Thus the transformation of the lines—which in the individual start to curve and then close in a circle to form the design of an eye—repeats in abridged form the evolutionary transformation of the species. Some pages later, comparing several different caterpillars of the genus *Deilephila* (of the family *Sphingidae*), Weismann writes again that "the oldest ancestors possessed only longitudinal stripes" from which "small pieces were cut off as ring-spots, and these were gradually perfected and ultimately duplicated, while at the same time the original marking, the longitudinal stripe, was shunted back further and further in the young stages, until it finally disappeared altogether."

By observing the individual development (ontogenesis) of these caterpillars, we are therefore also witnessing a sped-up version of the changes to these lines and shapes which might have taken tens of millions of years to draw themselves (the first lepidoptera fossils appear to date to the Lower Jurassic period, about 190 million years ago).[32]

After this brief detour via the ontogenesis and phylogenesis of these mimetic caterpillars, we can better

32 David Grimaldi and Michael S. Engel, eds., *Evolution of the Insects* (Cambridge: Cambridge University Press, 2005), p. 556.

understand the meaning of neoteny and heterochronicity more generally. So let's return to Simondon and his discussion of "mental images" or "image-objects."

The Moltings of the Image

In the passage that caught our attention, Simondon suggests that images, from their "neotenic state"—that is, of being premature or incomplete—tend toward an "imaginal stage." In other words, there's a moment in the life of an image that corresponds to that of the larval or "embryonic" state of a living being ("embryo" is Simondon's word, to which I'll return before long). This larval image is expected to subsequently develop to yield "adult images." And so his term "imaginal stage" is precisely equivalent to this "completed adult stage."[33]

Ever since Linnaeus, naturalists have called the final stage in the development of a being that undergoes diverse metamorphoses the "imago."[34] In lepidoptera, for instance, the imago is the butterfly that the caterpillar (the larval stage) becomes by passing through the chrysalis stage (as a nymph) when it transforms. There's something strangely redundant in Simondon's

33 Simondon, *Imagination and Invention*, 18–19.

34 It's worth asking why Linnaeus, when he employed the term *imago* for the first time in what would become its accepted scientific usage to denote the last phase of the metamorphosis of insects (Linnaeus, *Systema naturae*, I, ii, 12th ed. [Stockholm: Laurentius Salvius, 1767], pp. 534–5), seized on a Latin word previously used to designate those molded wax death masks of aristocratic families' deceased ancestors. Simondon mentions the funerary traditions of ancient Rome and "the portraits, statues, and *imagines* of ancestors" (p. 132).

lexical choice to speak about the imago—the "imaginal stage"—of the image. But this tautological effect is only superficial. If it can be an embryo, it's because the image is not yet wholly the image that it is. And if we can say that it subsequently develops until it attains an adult state, it is because it becomes entirely the image that it had not yet been. The imago of the image, the imaginal stage of the image, would be the fully developed and accomplished image, the image entirely formed.

These formulations certainly have the advantage of bringing out, in an astonishing manner, the heterochronic character of images, their differential temporality or tonality (the fact that images are either ahead of or behind themselves, a bit like Peter Schlemihl chasing his shadow). But this way of putting things also has the defect of assuming a goal, a teleology that directs this process of iconogenesis. For Simondon, the image—simultaneously grasped as a tendency and a tensor (a *-tenic* stretching)—is destined to pass through a genetic cycle that has a determined outcome. This iconogenetic cycle has three phases: (1) The image initially exists in a "free state," or an unlinked state; it "develops for itself" as an "embryonic motor activity and perception." Simondon evokes the example of movements during dreams (Lucretius, he says, "noticed them in sleeping dogs"), and he describes a primary phase in the formation of images during which they are floating—not yet attached to a final end, not yet enrolled in an action oriented toward a specific end.[35] (2) Then, over the course

35 Simondon, *Imagination and Invention*, 32. In *De rerum natura*, book IV, lines 991–6, Lucretius speaks about sleeping "hunters' hounds" who will "give sudden yelps and keep snuffing the air, as if they were following the newly discovered tracks of wild animals; and often, when awakened, they pursue illusive

of the next, intermediate phase of iconogenesis, "images become effectively and directly functional": they are linked to objects perceived in the environment and also become linked between each other, that is, "they self-organize and self-stabilize in internally correlated groups according to the degree of relationship between the organism and its environment."[36] (3) Finally, at the end of the third phase, the images Simondon dubs "adults" self-aggregate to create "a mental world" where they refer to each other "according to a systematic mode of connections," which comes to constitute "a saturated universe."[37]

In this last phase, the aggregated images (both within and by the living subject) become what Simondon calls "symbols." Under that heading, they seem to regain, albeit at a superior level of organization or saturation, something of their original independence and disconnection, as in the free oneiric productions of dogs observed by Lucretius. Extending a metaphor taken from the lexicon of heraldry, Simondon proposes that we think of the image as "issuant"—that is, emerging from or detaching itself from the subject while also remaining partially within it (like those halfway-visible lions in certain blazons)—until it then becomes "passant," that is, displayed in its full autonomy and in full outline.[38]

---

semblances of stags (*cervorum simulacra*), as though they saw them in flight, until the delusion is dispelled and they recover their senses." Lucretius, *On the Nature of Things*, trans. Martin Ferguson Smith (Indianapolis: Hackett, 2001), p. 127.

36 Ibid., 19.

37 Ibid., 21.

38 The viscount Ludovic de Magny, in his *La Science du blason accompagnée d'un armorial général des familles nobles de l'Europe* (Paris: Institut héraldique, 1858), p. cxxiii, defines

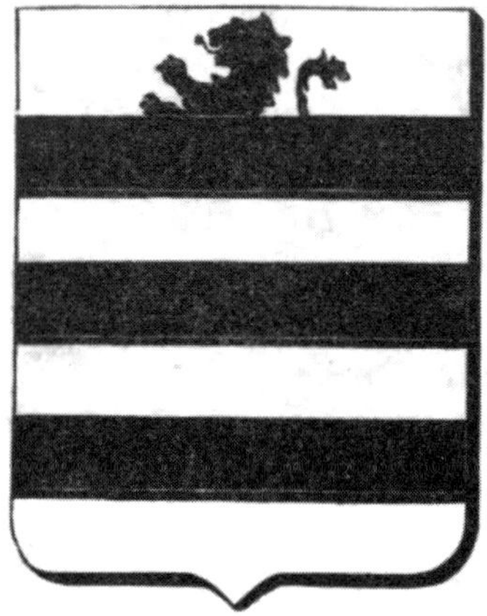

Issuant Lion, in Ludovic de Magny, La Science du blason accompagnée d'un armorial général des familles nobles de l'Europe *(Paris: Institut héraldique, 1858).*

The image, he concludes, is "formalized into a symbol by losing its links as a dated and personal memory," thereby cutting ties with "the living being" and the lived experience at the heart of which it came to be structured.[39] The image has experienced a molting, leaving its skin behind, the envelope of the living being through which it was able to grow and metamorphose.

But this de-linking of the image that ceases to be the parasite of its living host in order to live its own life, this regained autonomy of the image, is once more but a stage. By his own admission, Simondon is renewing ties with the "Platonic critique of the arts" and affirms that the arts—just as magic does—"interrupt the cycle of the image and prevent it from reaching its state of completion."[40]

an animal *issant* as an animal whose foreparts only are visible and appear to be emerging from the escutcheon.

39 Simondon, *Imagination and Invention*, pp. 137–8.

40 Ibid.

This is because in the Simondonian theory of iconogenesis, the image is not destined to exist for itself. Its ultimate destination is to prepare the ground of "invention," that is to say, the coming-into-the-world of an original object or technological device around which a saturated imaginal universe will reorganize itself, thus entailing "the recommencement of a new cycle." At the end of the day, Simondon considers the metamorphoses of images, from their embryonic stages to their adult form, to be only a transitional process directed toward the creation of objects, whether that be for humans or animals.[41] And "art" is the name of that which puts a stop to the iconogenetic cycle, preventing the image from attaining its own self-overcoming in the form of a technological invention. Art interrupts this cycle in an untimely manner, says Simondon, who goes so far as to suggest, following Plato, that art produces an unnatural inversion.[42]

---

41 "It is this relative exteriority [of the image in each of its stages] that is realized in invention by the position of created objects serving as organizers of the milieu. A created object is not a materialized image, nor is it placed arbitrarily in the world like an object among other objects in order to overload nature with an artificial supplement; it is (through its origin) and remains (through its function) a linkage system between the living and its milieu ... We can oppose neither human constructive operations to those practiced by animals, nor the fabrication of instruments smaller than the organism and borne by it to the setting up of roads, paths, storerooms, or limits in a territory serving as milieu to the organism, and thus larger than it. The tool and the instrument, just as much as paths and protections, are part of the envelope of the individual and mediate its relation to the milieu." Ibid., p. 186.

42 "The cycle of the image cannot be reversed," Simondon writes, before claiming that the arts, in Plato's critique, sought

Such a cycle—that of the life of the image—therefore seems destined to reabsorb the theoretical potential of the heterochronic tendency that Simondon had first opened for us. A heterochronicity predestined to be absorbed by that which it makes possible is necessarily relegated to a secondary or derivative status. The heterochronic component that distends the image—its neoteny, its prolonged embryonic state—works ultimately (i.e., at the end of its process of becoming and in the very name of a residual teleology) toward the accomplishment of a transformation in which it will annul itself.

One could certainly speak of "an ecology of images" in Simondon's work, that is, a way of thinking about images based on the relation between organism and environment.[43] And to the extent that the image is teleologically oriented toward the specific end of technological invention, this ecology of images is also an economy of images (an iconomy), in which the cyclical circulation of images is regulated by the rarity of what is useful. The cycle of the image, we read, "is a genesis that is marked in each of its stages by a sedimentation, a reduction in the number of elements preserved." In the passage from the first to the second phase of the cycle, "not all motor tendencies receive a confirmation of a

---

precisely "to rediscover an existence from symbols [i.e., to connect the image back to the subject from which it had been severed], inverting a becoming whose completion can only be found in invention … and not in an inversion of the cycle already accomplished." Ibid., p. 137.

43 Simondon himself does not use the term. "Ecology" is a word that almost never appears in his work—one remarkable exception being a 1983 article titled "Trois perspectives pour une réflexion sur l'éthique et la technique," republished in Simondon, *Sur la technique* (Paris: PUF, 2014), pp. 341–5.

perceptual experience"; from the intermediate phase to the final stage of the cycle, "only a few" images that have structured themselves via the subject they have inhabited "are formalized into symbols in order to organize the world of the imaginary serving as basis for invention."[44]

Simondonian iconogenesis appears to be a management of excess oriented toward an end.[45] So it would hardly be an exaggeration to describe it in the terms my great-uncle Imre was questioning: as an economic management of nature's house.

Toward a Radical Heterochronicity

Is that what we were looking for in the name of "an ecology of images"? No. We're attempting instead to plot a path toward a heterochronicity worthy of the name—a structural heterochronicity, not just an accidental offshoot of a process—one that opens at the heart of those images produced by nature, those images that we've been calling (in a more general sense) "acheiropoetic," not made by human hands. This is why, having listened to the promises and attended to the limits of

44 Simondon, *Imagination and Invention*, p. 138.

45 This teleology (or utility) and scarcity (or economy) at work in the cycle of image production appears quite clearly when Simondon describes the manner in which the neotenic image (triggering movement after the fashion of the dreaming dogs) is linked to perception: "The most primitive living beings execute a great number of movements which come to nothing because their perceptual apparatus is too undeveloped to direct these movements and endow them with efficacy, finality, and economy; the motor apparatus is in advance of the sensorial apparatus." Ibid., pp. 30–1.

Simondon's idea of a *-tenic* stretching of images, we will return to the phenomena of mimicry that we already briefly considered in those caterpillars studied by August Weismann, their stripes and their ocelli.

Contrary to Simondon's household or economic model for managing the surfeit of images, Roger Caillois insists on the uselessness, the pure aneconomic expenditure of images in his writings dedicated to different species' mimetic practices. *The Mask of Medusa*, published in 1960, is a veritable treatise on mimetology.[46] Guided by the idea of a generalized aesthetics beyond the human, Caillois never stops insisting that "mimicry is useless if not deleterious," that it's "a luxury," an "excess of simulacra." For Caillois, there are fundamentally *too many images, even in nature*: the iconomy of mimicry, such as he understands it, is close to the "general economy" of Georges Bataille, orientated toward superabundance.[47]

Even beyond his persistent critique of any teleology in the service of a "vital interest" or the "survival of the

46 [Translator's note: Caillois's book in French has the charming title of *Méduse et Cie*, literally "Jellyfish and Co." An out-of-print English translation from the 1960s opted for the more mythically portentous *The Mask of Medusa*. Although resonance with the Greek gorgon is intended and also built into the everyday French word for jellyfish, the title of Caillois's treatise on mimicry chiefly refers to the marine animal, and his critique of a natural economy implied by the ironically commercial "and Co." Instead of quoting from the English edition, I have retranslated the quotations from the French.]

47 Roger Caillois, *Méduse et Cie* (Paris: Gallimard, 1960), p. 113. See also p. 42, where the wings of the butterfly are "a luxury ornament"; or p. 51, where Caillois speaks of "an enormous squandering" and an ostentatious "expenditure." We will return in a later section to Bataille's concept of a "general economy."

species," what I want to retain from Caillois are essentially those moments when he stops, as if distracted, to consider the temporality or the tempo of animal mimicry. *The Mask of Medusa* emphasizes the importance of "immobility" that accompanies mimetic practices as well as the immense slowdown that makes of mimicry what Caillois terms "fashion in slow motion with variants that take millenia rather than seasons." This is the opposite of fashions and styles among humans, which are "rapid and whimsical." Among insects, "a single variation ... perpetuates itself, unchanging, with a longevity that human rhythms can only try to represent, at best painfully."[48]

In a famous article for the journal *Minotaure*, published in 1935, Caillois already saw mimicry—since it is "directed toward immobility and a return to the inorganic"—as a slowing down, a temporary freeze or rewind of evolution: "*Life takes a step backward*," he writes in italics next to a photograph of a giant phasmid (stick insect) that shows the rigidified creature almost wholly indistinguishable from a branch. The animal, imitating the plant, tends even toward the mineral.[49] Mimicry would thus be a sort of freeze-frame, or even better: *the image as freeze*.

Insomuch as it's a way of producing images that imply a transfer or borrowing of shapes and colors, mimicry according to Caillois calls for terms borrowed from the field of mediality, if one understands the concept of medium in its technological sense, or from the field of

48 Ibid., 97–8.

49 Roger Caillois, "Mimétisme et psychasthénie légendaire," *Minotaure* 7 (1935), p. 9; published in English as "Mimicry and Legendary Psychasthenia," trans. John Shepley, *October* 31 (1984), p. 30.

mediumnity, if one understands it in a parapsychological sense. The article in *Minotaure* describes mimicry as a kind of "teleplasty" (the word is borrowed from Frederic Myers, a theoretician of spiritualism, who used it to name the phenomenon of materializing at a distance). In the more complete version of Caillois's essay, included three years later in the anthology *Myth and Man*, the term "telephotography" is used to refer to the means by which an animal transposes on its own skin the retinal image of its surroundings. This time, the term is taken from the physiologist Jacques Loeb, who suggested it in a 1912 study of fish that blend in with the seabed.[50]

By considering mimicry through the prisms of parapsychology, photography, and fashion, Caillois pulls at the concept, extending and distending it between two temporalities. The first, a long or deep time, is that of the evolution of species; the second, volatile and fluctuating, is that of human creation and invention. But these contrasting rhythms are not only metaphorical. They are not simply the effects of word choice and tropes to describe the phenomenon of mimicry. In *The Mask of Medusa* he notes that "today, in the outskirts of large cities the wings of butterflies are slowly blackening," and thereby allows a glimpse of an evolutionary tempo that's effectively stretched between its long duration and the

50 Ibid., p. 7; see also Roger Caillois, *Le Mythe et l'homme* (Paris: Gallimard, 1938), p. 105. Frederic Meyers proposes the term "teleplastic" on the occasion of his discussion of the work of Alexander Aksakof. Frederic Meyers, "Review of A. Aksakof's *Animismus und Spiritismus*," *Proceedings of the Society for Psychical Research* 6 (1890), p. 669. And Jacques Loeb speaks of "telephotography" in "Die Bedeutung der Anpassung der Fische an den Untergrund für die Auffassung des Mechanismus des Sehens," *Zentralblatt für Physiologie* 25, no. 2 (January 1912), p. 1017.

environmental disruptions caused by industrialization.[51] The British entomologist James William Tutt was the first to suggest, already in 1896, that the wings of certain moths had turned black in order to better blend with tree trunks darkened by industrial soot.[52] Among other animals, such as the chameleon or a number of flatfish mentioned by Caillois in *The Mask of Medusa*, skin color changes almost instantaneously in order to "coincide with the general design of the surface on which the animal lives." Natural iconogenesis thus varies along a vast scale of durations, from longest to shortest. And mimicry also appears to be a matter of transferential velocities: in the manner of paleontologists who speak of bradytely and tachytely to designate slow or fast evolutions of species, we may refer to *bradyplasty* or *tachyplasty* to denote the tempi of the organic development of the image.[53]

---

51 Ibid., 106.

52 Cf. James William Tutt, *British Moths* (London: George Routledge & Sons, 1896), p. 305. The author explains that the peppered moth is "speckled" in order to blend in with the tree trunks it rests on, but, he continues, "near our large towns where there are factories, and where vast quantities of soot are day by day poured out from countless chimneys ... this Peppered Moth has, during the last fifty years, undergone a remarkable change. The white has entirely disappeared, and the wings have become totally black." The experiments conducted by the British geneticist Michael Majerus before his death in 2009 on this phenomenon known as "industrial melanism" seems to have confirmed Tutt's intuitions. (Majerus's results were published posthumously by a group of scientists in "Selective Bird Predation on the Peppered Moth: The Last Experiment of Michael Majerus," *Biology Letters* 8, no. 4 (2012), pp. 609–12.)

53 In his notes for a course at the Collège de France on "Nature," Maurice Merleau-Ponty proposes thinking about

A Pure Differential

Caillois's mimetology certainly presents a multiplicity of temporalities at work in iconogenesis, but nothing that states that the mimetic image, once formed, is heterochronic *in its very makeup*. Put another way: the organic development of an image comports with contrasting evolutionary and biological rates and rhythms, but the resulting image does not necessarily maintain active traces of these contrasts. Nothing indicates that the image ought to be considered as a stabilized differential.

Our current train of thought has now dropped us off in front of a problem that we might formalize like this: Caillois's analysis of mimeticism lacks a certain tension and intensity, that same tensility [*ténie*] that Simondon discovered in the image's becoming, even though he placed the (neo)tenic image under the authority of a functionalist, end-oriented economy that ultimately deprived the image of its integrity [*sa tenue propre*]. This is why, after Simondon and Caillois, we are left with a stubborn question: Can one think about the so-called natural image (acheiropoetic in the largest sense)

"bradytely" and "tachytely," concepts he took from the work of the American paleontologist George Gaylord Simpson, *Tempo and Mode in Evolution* (New York: Columbia University Press, 1944), in the context of what he calls "evolutionary kinetics." Merleau-Ponty also devotes several remarkable pages to mimicry that mesh, at many points, with Caillois's analyses. "We must criticize the assimilation of the notion of life with the notion of the pursuit of utility or an intentional project. The animal's form is not the manifestation of a teleology … What the animal displays is not utility, its appearance manifests something that more closely resembles our dream-life." Merleau-Ponty, *La Nature: Notes, cours du Collège de France*, ed. Dominique Séglard (Paris: Seuil, 1995), pp. 246, 315–16.

as "tensive"—as if stretched by a tone or tonality that is not already a tendency toward some goal or state determined ahead of time? Can one think the image as a pure differential, as a heterochronicity without a programmed reabsorption?

A phenomenon described by Edward Poulton in 1890 and sometimes designated as "automimicry" might put us on the right path. Speaking about the ocelli and false antennae that decorate the rear portion of the wings of the butterfly known as the grey hairstreak, Poulton explains that they produce the deceptive appearance of a head "*at the wrong end of the body*."[54]

---

54 Edward Bagnall Poulton, *The Colours of Animals: Their Meaning and Use* (London: Kegan Paul, 1890), p. 207. To speak of "automimicry" in cases of this type is certainly a rare usage of the term. But one finds it, for instance, in the brief study that Russell Dale Guthrie and Ronald Petocz devoted to the mimetic relation between the black stripes created by the inner ear fur of particular antelopes and the grooves on the horns of the same antelopes, "Weapon Automimicry Among Mammals," *American Naturalist* 104, no. 940 (1970); or again in Simcha Lev-Yadun's interpretation of the parts of certain species of agave and aloe plants that imitate their own thorns, "Weapon (Thorn) Automimicry and Mimicry of Aposematic Colorful Thorns in Plants," *Journal of Theoretical Biology* 224, no. 2 (2003). In the majority of scientific studies, however, the term is reserved for the imitation of different members of the same species that are endowed with superior means of defense. See Graeme Ruxton, Thomas Sherratt, and Michael Speed, *Avoiding Attack: The Evolutionary Ecology of Crypsis, Warning Signals, and Mimicry* (Oxford: Oxford University Press, 2004), p. 176. When Caillois speaks about mimicry in general as an "autoplastic energy" that grants to insects "that strange ability to remodel their own appearance" (*Méduse et Cie*, p. 99), he takes the term "autoplastic" from the surgeon Philippe Frédéric Blandin, author of a treatise titled *Autoplastie ou restauration*

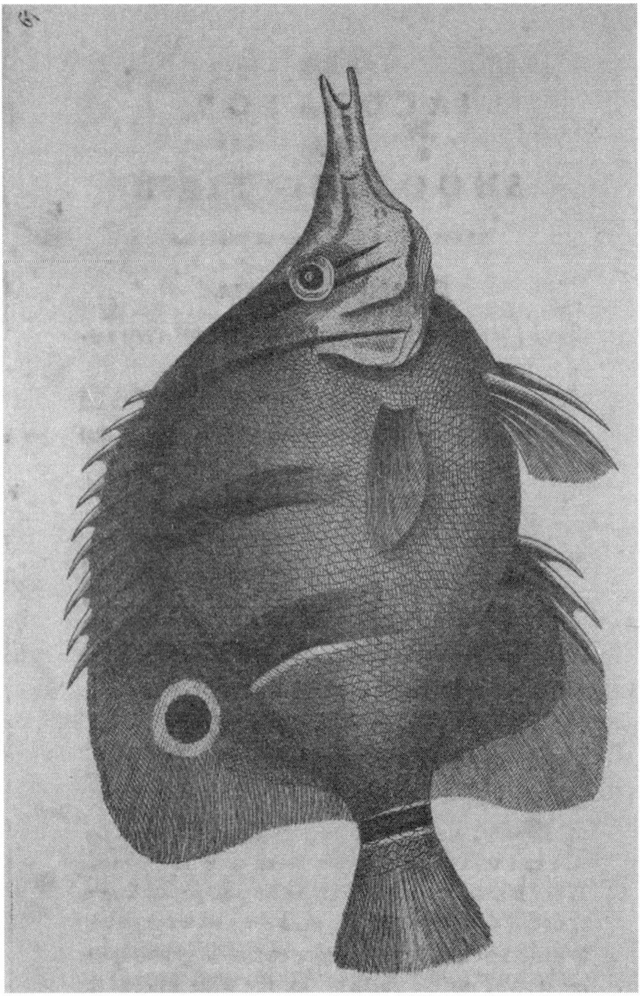

Four-eye butterflyfish, in George Shaw and Frederick Nodder, Naturalist's Miscellany, *vol. 2 (London: Nodder & Co, 1790).*

This self-imitation, at least of a part of oneself in this case, is the reason why I'm calling this kind of production *automimetic*. The being in question in some way folds itself in order to duplicate itself, becomes a partial mirror of itself. And in this way it produces, simultaneously, a difference with itself. It's as if by seeking to create an identical copy of itself, the butterfly in fact succeeds in reinventing the placement of its head. We can say the same thing about the foureye butterflyfish, whose scientific name is *Chaetodon capistratus*: it reproduces an image of its own eyes on its skin, displacing them elsewhere. The butterfly or the fish that self-mimics ends up dissembling itself the better it resembles itself, or it comes to resemble itself the more it dissembles itself.

If we consider these automimetic beings as so many images produced over the course of a natural iconogenesis, then we must also say that such images are the stabilized result of a movement of self-differentiation, of a gap between self and self. Another head—the same—another eye—the same—have been traced, drawn, formed, after (in both senses) their model, modeled little by little after itself, so that the being in question finds itself *behind or ahead of itself*, to the exact extent that it is in the process of conforming with itself. It does not yet have the head or the eye that it *already has*. Of course, the advance or the delay is measured here on

des parties du corps qui ont été détruites à la faveur d'un emprunt fait à d'autres parties plus ou moins éloignées (Paris: Germer Baillière, 1836). All the same, Caillois pays no attention to automimicry in the way that it interests me here: at the most, for him, automimicry is just one technique among others that "diverts an attack … on the vital organs of animal (usually the head and eyes) toward less important parts of the body" (*Méduse et Cie*, p. 73).

the scale of millions of years of evolution, but, in their principles, these acts of automimicry follow a pattern of heterochronicity that we have already seen in the figure of Peter Schlemihl running after his shadow.

(To those who might here be tempted to object that we're only talking about some peculiar cases and that automimicry, a rather exceptional phenomenon in the realm of living beings, cannot serve to confirm a *general* hypothesis about organic iconogenesis characterized by heterochronicity, I will risk suggesting this: Isn't there an automimicry implied in any mimicry and thus in any organic iconogenesis? To resemble something or someone, with the time and energy that this takes, is to force oneself to become like something in the self that is already related to the other. It is to work toward the direction of that which in the self already differs from the self.)

Another phenomenon might equally help us think about heterochronicity—understood as that tensility or tension within self-differentiation—as it works in the natural image. It's a question here of cases that are somehow symmetrical with those that we've just looked at, since this time, rather than differentiating oneself by imitating oneself, mimetic configuration is undertaken and takes shape precisely *in the absence of a model*, that is, after the disappearance of the model. Two American biologists recently studied the evolution of mimicry in the scarlet kingsnake (*Lampropeltis elapsoides*), a nonvenomous species of snake that, to discourage its predators, imitates an extremely venomous coral snake (*Micrurus fulvius*): around 1960, the latter disappeared from the region cohabited by the two species (the Sandhills of North Carolina), after which the mimic snake started to *look even more like its henceforth-unfindable model*. It's as if once the mimetic process was unleashed, it began to work for itself without a given referent.[55]

I said that this example of mimicry in absentia—or modeling without a model—is symmetrical with automimicry: rather than differentiating from oneself in the very movement of conforming with oneself, the scarlet kingsnake becomes ever more identical with another who no longer exists.

In the same vein, I should mention here two fictional or speculative cases proposed by Vladimir Nabokov, himself a noted entomologist, specializing in butterflies. The writer had imagined a sequel to his novel *The Gift*, in which the narrator's father is a butterfly collector and author of articles criticizing Darwin's theory of evolution. In the pages published after the death of Nabokov, we come across the case of a caterpillar of his own invention (*Pseudodemas tschumarae*) that mimics the flowers of an equally imaginary plant (*Tschumara vitimensis*), but one of these, the caterpillar, appears at the end of summer, whereas the plant flowers only in May. The mimic and its model perfectly miss each other; they are forever out of phase, their paths crossing without them ever actually meeting.

---

55 Christopher Akcali and David Pfenning, "Rapid Evolution of Mimicry Following Local Model Extinction," *Biology Letters* 10, no. 6 (2014), p. 4: "Paradoxically, selection imposed on mimics by predators can generate an 'evolutionary momentum' towards more precise mimicry—even after models go extinct." This form of mimicry—where an inoffensive species scares off its predators by mimicking a species that is dangerous for them—is known as Batesian mimicry. Henry Walter Bates was the first to describe it in his "Contributions to an Insect Fauna of the Amazon Valley," *Transactions of the Linnean Society of London* 23, no. 3 (1862), pp. 495–566.

This temporal rift between the model and the mimic—their missed encounter—prefigures another speculative moment in the text that has the stated ambition to critique any strictly Darwinian and gradualist concept of mimicry between species. A continuous and constant evolution, the narrator says, cannot possibly explain the improbable fact of a visual convergence between separate species, because nowhere are to be found those "transitional forms"—that is, relative similarities, still imperfect, still in a state of becoming. If mimetic assimilation must be produced insensibly, the narrator continues, if it comes into being little by little by "a gradual accumulation of corresponding traits," even then "a trillion light years would hardly be sufficient." And here the narrator throws himself into a funny and vertiginous meditation on the multiple temporalities that are woven into the framework of organic iconogenesis:

> The time span might be sufficient, but only on condition that the species developing a "protective mimicry" ... were pursuing this goal consciously, having conferred beforehand with the model and determined that the latter, during the full number of centuries required by the toiler at evolution toward a gradual attainment of resemblance, would remain unchanged (in the kind of immobility that a painter demands of his model). The process would accelerate further if the model just as consciously indulged the imitator by mutating part way in proportion to the mime's mutations, or if the very goal of the imitator were to change concomitantly with the evolutionary metamorphoses of the model, in the same way a painter, having begun a nude of a young female model, might strive for a likeness with such ardor that, as he tirelessly recorded every trait, he would, in the end,

> find that he was depicting the old woman into which the model had evolved during her plurennial pose.[56]

What is conveyed by these long sentences of Nabokov's narrator with their meandering propositional clauses, their sinuous asides, their parentheses? Where are they taking us in their "inchworm progress," as the narrator refers to the style of his father's entomological writings? What the narrator demonstrates by a kind of reductio ad absurdum is that mimetic iconogenesis produces dissemblance at the very heart of resemblance, and vice versa. I'll explain myself. On the one hand, the very ardor of the drive to imitate leads to the production of something other than the intended object of reproduction (the painter who overscrupulously paints his young female model ends up depicting an old woman). On the other hand, if resemblance is not generated by gradual mimetic convergence, then it can only be the result of a hitch, a leap, a hiatus, or a sudden dissembling.

But we must take one more step and say that it's the divergence of speeds that produces both resemblance as dissemblance *and* dissemblance as resemblance. Indeed, the perfect imitation of the other (the painter depicting his model) becomes a dissimilitude precisely *because of the time it would take* (the model will have changed in the meantime, as if the potter's daughter from Pliny ends up, by trying to be too careful, tracing the silhouette of her lover as an old man). Put differently,

56 Vladimir Nabokov, "Fathers Butterflies," in *Nabokov's Butterflies*, ed. Brian Boyd and Robert Michael Pyle, trans. Dmitri Nabokov (Boston: Beacon, 2000), p. 224. On the fictional character of the said caterpillar and plant, see Peter Forbes, *Dazzled and Deceived: Mimicry and Camouflage* (New Haven, CT: Yale University Press, 2009), p. 130.

it is for the sake of resemblance that resemblance is belated. But conversely, if resemblance can only be born from the unexpected gap introduced by dissemblance, then resemblance also runs ahead of time: a being that we suddenly realize looks like another different being already resembles this other without even having the time to gradually become similar.

What we find in Nabokov's fiction about lepidoptera and mimicry is the quintessential formulation of the heterochronicity of the natural or organic image. In the enlarged perspective of a nonhuman iconomy, the image really henceforth appears as the differential of the temporalities that pull at it, stretch it, that give it its tone, its tensility [*ténie*]. The image quavers, held within an irresolvable and undiminished dissonance.

Interlude:
The Accident of Slow Motion

Imagine that an accident happened one day during what we might call the universal history of the image: the invention of slow motion.

It seems that the first slo-mo in the history of cinema, in 1894, was indeed filmed accidentally by William Dickson, a Scottish inventor working in Thomas Edison's laboratory on the kinetograph. It's a thirty-second sequence of the Venezuelan acrobat Juan Caicedo dancing on a tightrope.

The shooting was done outside because the dimensions of the Black Maria—the name bestowed upon the first studio in cinema because of its walls covered in tar paper—were insufficient for the length of rope. As reported in an article at the time, "It is the first time that any kinetographic pictures have been taken in the open air, and the results were looked forward to with interest."[1]

The acrobat was thus filmed in broad daylight, which posed a problem: the adjustable diaphragm had not yet been invented. Dickson had the idea to speed up the

1 "Signor Caicedo's Fine Exhibition," *Orange Chronicle*, July 28, 1894; quoted on the webpage of the National Film Preservation Foundation (filmpreservation.org) dedicated to this short clip known as *Caicedo (with Pole)* or *Caicedo, King of the Slack Wire*.

camera: rolling at forty images per second instead of the usual sixteen or eighteen at that time. In order to reduce the amount of light he had to reduce the exposure time of each section of film. When the images obtained in this way were projected at the normal rate, it created a slightly slowed motion. The result was that the funambulist's ballet gained something even more airy and ethereal. It had undergone what Jean Epstein would later term "a dramatic surrealizing." The scarcely perceptible slowing down of the dancer's gestures "prolongs and holds them in suspense."[2]

The accident of slow motion that occurred on that fine day in 1894 has since been reproduced countless times. The Austrian priest and physician August Musger filed a patent on the mechanism in 1904. But it was Hans Lehmann, director of the research and development department of the Dresden firm Ernemann, who claimed, without crediting Musger, to be the inventor when he presented it to the public in 1914, then boasted of its advantages in a 1917 article titled "Time's magnifying glass." In the same way that the invention of the microscope had enlarged objects in three dimensions, slow motion would enlarge objects in the fourth dimension, time.[3]

In 1928, when Jean Epstein mentions slow motion in his writings—at the same time that he illustrated, in arresting fashion, its use in his film adaptation of

2 Jean Epstein, "The Delirium of a Machine," trans. Christophe Wall-Romana, in *Jean Epstein: Critical Essays and New Translations*, ed. Sarah Keller and Jason N. Paul (Amsterdam: Amsterdam University Press, 2012), p. 375; and Epstein, "Dramaturgy in Time," trans. Audrey Brunetaux, in ibid., p. 351.

3 Hans Lehmann, "Die Zeitlupe," *Die Umschau* 21, no. 22 (1917), pp. 426–30.

Edgar Allan Poe's "The Fall of the House of Usher"—he sees it above all as adding "a new dramaturgical register." Rather than an expansion of time, it permits a "dramatic enlargement." Epstein describes this in a fascinating account of slow motion's effects on human facial expressions:

> I know of nothing so utterly moving as a facial expression liberated by slow motion. There's an entire preliminary preparation, a slow fever, which it's hard to know whether to compare to a morbid growth, a gradual maturation, or even more vulgarly, a pregnancy. Finally, this whole effort overflows and the stiffness of muscle melts. A contagion of movement passes over the face. Eyelash tips and base of chin pulse in the same rhythm. And once the lips separate at last to indicate a scream, we will have been present at every moment of the cry's long and magnificent dawning.[4]

In his later essays, Epstein will decouple slow motion from human affects and see the technology operating over a much wider range. Considered from the standpoint of the natural history of the image, slow motion isn't that different from Caillois's mimicry. As we recall from the *Minotaure* article cited in the previous chapter, mimicry acts as a sort of rewind of evolution, making life pass in reverse, from animal to vegetable to mineral. In his 1946 *The Intelligence of a Machine*, Epstein notes that in slow motion the clumsiness normally inherent in human gestures disappears and is absorbed into "the infallible grace of animal instinct." In this vein, he continues:

---

4 Jean Epstein, "L'Âme au ralenti" (1928), in *Écrits sur le cinéma*, vol. 1 (Paris: Seghers, 1974), p. 191.

> Regression reaches even further, beyond the animal stage. It rediscovers, in the movements of the torso or the neck, the active elasticity of the stem; in the undulating of hair or a horse mane, the swaying of a forest; in the beating of fins and wings, the palpitating of leaves; in the coiling and uncoiling of reptiles, the spiral sense of all vegetal growth. Slowed down even more, any living substance goes back to its fundamental viscosity and lets its deep colloidal nature rise to the surface. Finally, when there is no longer any visible movement in a sufficiently stretched time, humans become statues, the living merges with the inert, the universe devolves into a desert of pure matter without any trace of spirit.[5]

Slow motion is emancipated from the human figure in order to become a universal phenomenon that Epstein will soon endow with a new name. In "The Fluid World of the Screen," an essay first published in *Les Temps modernes* in 1950, Epstein—who also compares the filmic eye to "a mobile snail eye, an eye mounted on an extendable and retractable stem"—proposes the term "bradyscopy" as the temporal equivalent of "microscopy."[6] The word of course resembles the bradytely of paleontologists—that is, the slowdown to a point of stasis in the evolution of a species (what has since been called "living fossils," arrested at a stage that seems unchangeable, like coelacanths, those fish of the deeps which retain the vestiges of the lungs they had when

5 Jean Epstein, *The Intelligence of a Machine*, trans. Christophe Wall-Romana (Minneapolis: Univocal Publishing, 2014), p. 29.

6 Jean Epstein, "The Fluid World of the Screen," trans. Sarah Keller, in *Jean Epstein: Critical Essays and New Translations*, pp. 383, 385.

they lived closer to the surface, hundreds of millions of years ago).

But this filmic slowdown, which Epstein envisages on a universal scale, also brings us face to face with a temporal paradox that never ceases to amaze: at the same time that slow motion enlarges and distends the condensed durations of those movements and gestures that we're used to seeing and performing, it also appears to reduce and contract those immeasurable periods of natural history down to the scale of our own perception. We literally witness the passage from one kingdom to another (from animal to vegetable to mineral), although we are moving against the grain of evolution. In short, *by holding back movement, slow motion speeds it up*. By stretching out time, it precipitates and permits perception of extremely slow-moving shifts and mutations that once exclusively belonged to a geological temporality destined to escape us.

This is why slow motion, conceived in this way, pulls or stretches images between two diverging movements. The slow motion described by Epstein is another *differential of speeds*, as he himself suggests in his 1946 article titled "Dramaturgy in Time": thanks to this "discovery of temporal perspective" constituted by slow and fast motion in cinema, it has become "suddenly possible" to compare "several different speeds in the sequence of an event," and because "we only know things through their differences," only in comparison, Epstein adds, "in a world with a unique speed, time would disappear."[7] Which is to say that if there is time at all, it's because there is heterochronicity.

---

7 Epstein, "Dramaturgy in Time," p. 349.

The consequences of Epstein's intuition for thinking about time in general have yet to be explored in full. As far as what concerns us here—that is, the question of iconogenesis, conceived as a momentarily stabilized tension between differing speeds—Epstein's meditations on the accident of slow motion in the universal history of the image lead us to the following conclusion: just like the fixed image, the moving image is also a differential of time. In this way we can say, in a Deleuzian register, that any image, whether it be mobile or immobile, whether it bears a human stamp or is acheiropoetic, is a *differential-image*.

II

Iconomy on a Universal Scale

Let us set out again, this time beginning with an old image (from 1745): an engraving by William Hogarth titled *The Battle of the Pictures*. The inscription at the top suggests that we might be dealing with a piece of self-promotion: "The Bearer hereof is Entitled (if he thinks proper,) to be a Bidder for Mr. Hogarth's Pictures, which are to be sold on the Last day of this Month."

The picture we have on our hands here is thus a picture whose function permits the purchase of other pictures. It promises an exchange, if not exactly for another image (for which this one would effectively constitute payment), at least for the *possibility* of acquiring other images. This is a picture that both depicts and grants access to the picture market, to the place where pictures circulate and compete economically. In other words, this is an image of what I have been referring to as "an iconomy."

Commentators on and interpreters of Hogarth's work have attempted to decode this picture of (the conflict or exchange between) pictures. We can identify in the shadows on the right, displayed on an easel, *The Tête à Tête*, the second painting in Hogarth's *Marriage À-la-Mode* series, executed around 1743. That painting here is being slit by a reproduction of the famous *Aldobrandini Wedding*. We might also recognize the copy of a

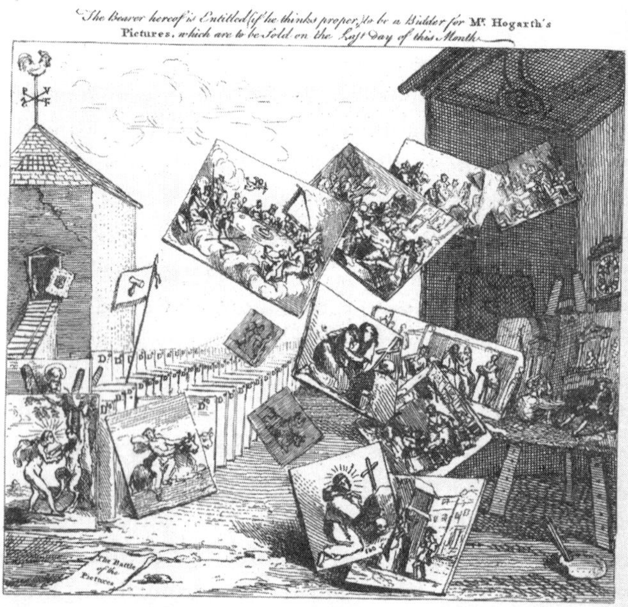

William Hogarth, The Battle of the Pictures, *engraving, 1745*

Saint Francis, its lower right corner intruding upon *Morning* from Hogarth's series *The Four Times of Day*, painted and then engraved in 1736 and 1738.[1]

But before we rush to recognize or identify anything, we should take note of the most striking thing about this engraving: there are no buyers, no viewers. There is literally *no one*, except at the top left, at the top of the stairs, the miniaturized figure of an auctioneer, so designated by his emblem, the hammer, on the flag that's planted in the middle of the field of canvases that extend to the horizon. Otherwise, there's no one apart from the paintings themselves, bumping, tearing, and scrapping with each other in a kind of aerial arena. The competition seems to be taking place among themselves, for themselves, *without us*: an acheiropoetic iconomy.

Beyond the context of eighteenth-century England and its art market, what might happen if we thought of this image as if it had fallen to Earth from some unknown time and place? Perhaps it would appear to us as a cross section or a fragment of the universal circulation of images, both up there and down here: not only on the earth—or even beneath the earth, if we think about the cables through which most of today's images transit—but also above us in the atmosphere and in extraterrestrial space where image-relaying satellites orbit.

Let us observe this image of the economy and traffic of images themselves, as if it were being drawn from a market of the visible with even greater dimensions than that which it depicts, the market of a general iconomy.

1 See, in particular, Thomas Clerk, *The Works of William Hogarth (Including the "Analysis of Beauty") Elucidated by Descriptions, Critical, Moral, and Historical; Founded on the Most Approved Authorities*, vol. 2 (London: R. Scholey, 1812), pp. 67–8.

Let us approach this engraving as if it permits us to see and to think about what we'll call—adapting a coinage of Georges Bataille's—*iconomy on a universal scale.*

The Gift of Sight: Iconomic Expenditure

Bataille has effectively challenged us to conceive of economics from an expanded point of view. In *The Accursed Share*, he suggests we think economically about "the movement of energy on the earth."[2] And several years earlier, in 1946, he devotes a series of notes to the idea of "an economy on a universal scale," an economics that would study "the living world as a whole."[3]

This generalization of the concept of economy means first of all changing the scale and expanding the strict frontiers in which the idea of economics is usually enclosed. I would like here to echo the question Bataille asks in the first chapter of *The Accursed Share*—"Isn't there a need to study the system of human production and consumption within a much larger framework?"[4]—and to ask also whether we should attempt to understand the circulation of images, which Hogarth's engraving shows us in tight focus, by resituating it within an economy enlarged to a universal dimension.

For Bataille, universal economics is distinguished from economics in its usual sense by thinking from

2 Georges Bataille, *The Accursed Share: An Essay on General Economy*, vol. 1, *Consumption*, trans. Robert Hurley (New York: Zone Books, 1988), p. 10.

3 Georges Bataille, "The Economy to the Proportion of the Universe" (1946), in *Georges Bataille: Essential Writings*, ed. Michael Richardson (London: SAGE, 1998), p. 75.

4 Bataille, *The Accursed Share*, p. 20.

"the perspective of the excess of energy:"[5] in general economy, he writes, "the 'expenditure' (the 'consumption') of wealth, rather than production, was the primary object."[6] Indeed, we should take pure waste or loss as the starting point for analysis. This type of excess has nothing to do with the surplus produced within a restricted economy of the capitalist type. That surplus is destined to be consumed only so that it might be reinscribed and reinvested within the cycle of wealth accumulation. Thus, in one of the abandoned fragments of the *Accursed Share*, we read that "capitalism didn't lead to the suppression of unproductive expenditures ... it tended to limit them to further consumption of its products."[7]

Already we can see how this works for our purposes: the economy of images shown in Hogarth's engraving is divided between these two perspectives. On the one hand, there's the regular market of images at the heart of which expenditure is regulated and contained. The scene in *The Battle of the Pictures* is that of the auction market where one seeks—sometimes in spectacular or

5 Bataille, "The Economy to the Proportion of the Universe," p. 77.

6 Bataille, *The Accursed Share*, p. 9.

7 Bataille, *La Limite de l'utile*, in *Oeuvres complètes*, vol. 7, p. 223; see also p. 231: "This tentacular system is distinguished from others by spending only on the condition of absorbing *more* than it loses ... Capital attains the greatest capacity of absorbing forces and can only deliver them by sucking in more than it puts out. This requires the existence of forces outside the capitalist system that are not yet reduced to it but ultimately reducible—whether these take the form of backward countries or unexploited fields of possibilities (resulting from new inventions). Should the system stop absorbing these new forces it would soon stop being able to deliver its products."

acrobatic fashion—the point of equilibrium between offer and proffer, the best price. But, on the other hand, the engraving also asks us to think about something else, through its near disappearance of human agents and its infinite multiplication of images (letting them proliferate until the image's own vanishing point). It takes us to the limits of the iconomic market and points to what lies beyond and outside it.

In "The Economy to the Proportion of the Universe," Bataille aims at "posing the economic problem against the grain," at "turning the usual perspective upside down" in order to consider "*a need the globe has to lose what it cannot contain.*"[8] The question inspired by Bataille that awaits us here is as follows: In the visual economy, what would amount to an expenditure for its own sake and at a total loss? Or, where and when do we begin to have images *for nothing*, images that are *lost to sight*?

But before we pull Bataille completely into this universal iconomy, we should stop a moment and consider those oft-remarked-upon paradoxical elements in his hypothesis. For Bataille's purpose was not merely to generalize a concept of economics that would otherwise remain intact, to expand it without changing it. With the notion of pure expenditure, the idea of the economic opens out onto something that might just as easily be characterized as aneconomic, since it would elude rational accounting in terms of returns or profitability.

These two contradictory movements, generalizing economics and also surpassing it, can be read *together* in a remarkable passage of *The Accursed Share*. Bataille starts off by regretting that the economy "is never

8 Bataille, "The Economy to the Proportion of the Universe," p. 77.

considered in *general*," that it remains confined to "*particular* systems (organisms or enterprises)." But he then adds that what restrains the field of "economic science" is that it remains content to consider operations only "with a view to a limited end," that it "does not take into consideration a play of energy that no particular end limits."[9] In a couple of sentences, Bataille simultaneously articulates both the generalization and dissolution of the economic within an aneconomic horizon that escapes the regime of utility, which is to say also the regime of ends—or at least human ends. The transition from economy in this restricted sense to a general, universal economy is necessarily accompanied by a rupture with anthropocentrism.[10]

9 Bataille, *The Accursed Share*, pp. 22–3.

10 See the remarkable little essay titled "Celestial Bodies" (1938), trans. Annette Michelson, *October* 36 (1986). Bataille opposes the "extraordinary loss" that characterizes the Sun (as an "incandescent star" that "lavishes its force in space," that gives without counting) and "the absence of radiation" that characterizes the earth (77–8). As one moves from the "central core" of the earth toward the earth's crust and the atmosphere, there is an "ever higher power [to] no longer expend, but rather consume." "The crowning achievement of this tendency is anthropocentrism," Bataille continues, since it completes this process of cooling that requires energy rather than giving energy: "The weakening of the terrestrial globe's material energy has enabled the constitution of the autonomous human existences which are so many misconceptions of the universe's movement. These existences may be compared to those of the feudal lord, who gains independence insofar as the central power ceases to have energetic action. But man's avidity, taken as a whole, is much greater than that of the local sovereign himself. The latter contents himself with preventing the king's agents from mixing in his affairs, while the human being loses awareness of the reality of his world—as the parasite

"A general economy": the expression itself seems aporetic in the final reckoning, that is to say, where reckoning and accounting are on the cusp of being interrupted, the point where economic rationality itself might be literally exceeded, beyond any potential generalization. What could remain of the economic impulse in a general economy that no longer calculates or expects any return on investment? Why then keep this name, this old name of "economy"?

This aporia haunts Bataille. We can see it even well before *The Accursed Share*, in the short 1933 text titled "The Notion of Expenditure." On the one hand, Bataille calls for the adoption of a perspective that we might term "meta-economic," since it puts into question "the fundamental value of the word *useful*" (the use of use, or the value of use value) along with "an *interest* in considerable losses" (the useless considered as a superior mode of investment). On the other hand, Bataille also asserts the radically aneconomic nature of pure consumption when he imagines a "principle of loss, in other words, of unconditional expenditure, no matter how contrary it might be to the economic principle of balanced accounts."[11]

But the knot of this aporia at work in Bataille's economic discourse is the gift. And we should pay it even more attention since, as we will see, what is at stake is above all a gift of light, that is, of visibility. The gift, as

---

is unaware of the pain or joy of those from whom it draws subsistence." Anthropomorphism, or anthropocentrism, is the effect of a forgetting or erasure of general economy.

11 Georges Bataille, "The Notion of Expenditure" (1933), in *Visions of Excess: Selected Writings, 1927–1939*, ed. Allan Stoekl (Minneapolis: University of Minnesota Press, 1985), pp. 116–18.

Bataille thinks of it, is essentially the gift of sight on the scale of the universe.

In a note, Bataille says explicitly that the idea for *The Accursed Share* began with his reading of Marcel Mauss's essay *The Gift*, a text devoted to the institution of the potlatch, that is, of those gifts that oblige the receiver to give in return even more than what they received, in the form of a counter-gift that raises the stakes of generosity. The potlatch itself becomes the site of this aporetic oscillation between excess beyond economic calculation (the pure gratuitous generosity of the giver) and the pursuit of a calculus according to a hypereconomy (gratuitousness and generosity themselves become a rivalry and a competition, so much so that giving becomes a kind of earning). As Bataille puts it, someone who can give like this "enriches himself with a contempt of riches."[12]

From the point of view of the general economy that interests us here, the potlatch is only one particular and anthropocentric version of the gift. Indeed, for Bataille, it's the sun who acts as the primary and unconditional giver: it "dispenses energy—wealth—without any return"; it "gives without ever receiving";[13] "*it loses itself without counting*."[14] The true gift worthy of the name —the only one that's unconditional and without expectation of some return on the initial investment—does it belong only to the day star? Is it solar energy that realizes what *The Accursed Share* calls "the ideal" of any gift, "that a potlatch could not be repaid?"[15]

12 Bataille, *The Accursed Share*, p. 69.

13 Ibid., p. 28.

14 Bataille, "The Economy to the Proportion of the Universe," p. 74.

15 Bataille, *The Accursed Share*, p. 70.

The gift of visibility, the gift of daylight—perhaps that is the place where, in Hogarth's engraving, all those images that multiply until they are lost to sight are leading us, toward the fountainhead of those gifts.

An Overflow of Images

Here we are, back in front of *The Battle of the Pictures*. Looking at this picture of the circulation of and competition between pictures, observing this meta-image, we notice all those frames, innumerable frames. They are squares (the French word for frame—*cadre*—comes from the Italian *quadro*) that multiply infinitely while attempting to box each other up. The engraving itself is in a square format, and inside its frame are framed these other square-framed canvases trying to contain other square frames.

I emphasize all these quadrilaterals and framings because the possibility of containing an entire circulation within a framework is exactly the thing that distinguishes economy in the usual sense from Bataille's general economy—that economy beyond economy, where pure expenditure can no longer be contained and leaks out everywhere.

The images in Hogarth's engraving appear simultaneously to want to leave the frame and to be under a compulsion to do so. They have become so numerous that they no longer fit inside it; they all press up against each other. And the images also seem to be seeking to liberate themselves from the restricted iconomic space confining them in order to light out for some kind of excess of unlimited movement that we will have to figure out.

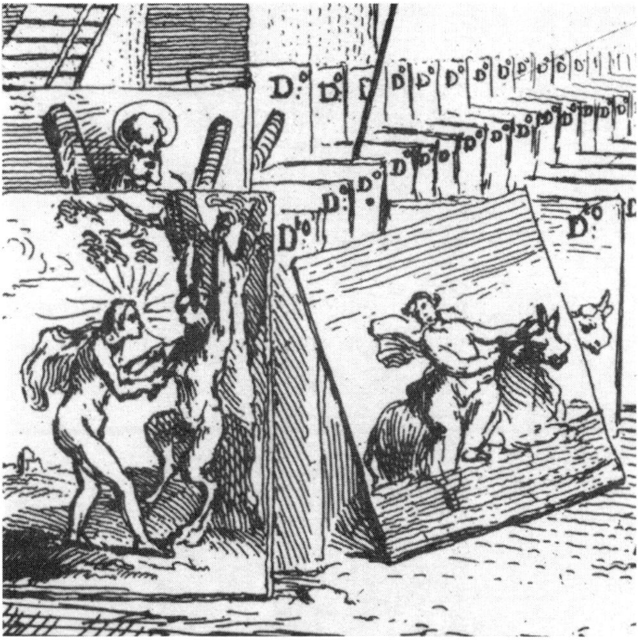

William Hogarth, The Battle of the Pictures, *engraving, 1745 (detail)*

Breaking the frame: this happens in at least three ways. Let's try to describe each one in turn.

1) Images infinitely proliferate toward the back of the engraving, as if the unstoppable multiplication of their reproductions requires them to shove the background back ever further, until the vanishing point. In each of those three ranks of images seen on the left, there are in fact simply innumerable copies of a single image. In the rank closest to the center of the picture, the theme of the rape of Europa by Zeus, the horns of the bull can be seen repeated in the second painting. Then, in the rank nearest the edge, we can see the repeated end

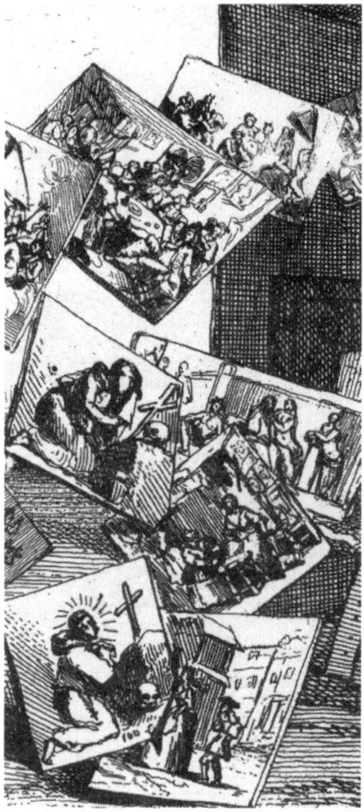

William Hogarth, The Battle of the Pictures, *engraving, 1745 (detail)*

of the branch of the cross where Saint Andrew is crucified. Further, there is mention everywhere of "D^{to}" (an abbreviation of "ditto"), confirming what we've already suspected: that behind each of the three scenes (the third is Apollo flaying Marsyas) are merely infinite replicas. Somehow, it's as if Hogarth had foreseen the image saturation that we are now witnessing. We are living in a space fully engorged with images (a "one hundred percent image space," as Walter Benjamin writes).[16]

16 Walter Benjamin, "Surrealism: The Last Snapshot of the European Intelligentsia," trans. Edmund Jephcott, in *Selected*

William Hogarth, The Battle of the Pictures, *engraving, 1745 (detail)*

2) Several images in Hogarth's engraving bump into each other, as if seeking to intermingle. Beyond the canonical interpretation, according to which the author set out to expose the war, or iconomic competition, between his art and the old masters (represented by those classical scenes of Europa, Marsyas, and Saint Andrew) that have been abundantly imitated,[17] we can literally see, in the spectacle it offers, a commotion that pushes or leads these flying images to break with their own coherence,

---

Writings, vol. 2, part 1 (Cambridge, MA: Harvard University Press, 1999), p. 217. I have given a detailed analysis of this Benjaminian notion of a saturated image-space in *The Supermarket of the Visible: Toward a General Economy of Images*, trans. Jan Plug (New York: Fordham University Press, 2019), pp. 51–4.

17 Cf. Thomas Clerk, *Works of William Hogarth*, p. 68.

to fly out of their frames, to intermix and contaminate each other in the heat of their general confluence.

3) Finally, there is at least one image (an Apollo flaying a Marsyas that the engraver has shadowed with vertical hatching) that has managed to rise above the ranks of its countless clones, taking flight, seeming not to seek out contact or exchange with any of the other images but, instead, to attempt a getaway. This centrifugal image—or, better, *iconofugal*—is running away, toward the background, and at a diagonal, toward the upper right hand corner of this oversaturated image space.

These three drives or impulses toward an exit from enframing—all three entirely clear in Hogarth's engraving—might be respectively characterized as swelling, interpenetration, and flight. As figures of excess or overflow and leakage, all three point toward what I'm calling—after Bataille—a general iconomy, of which *The Battle of the Pictures* would be the anticipation or model in miniature.

Hot Air Balloons, Pigeons, and Satellites

Such an iconomic space, saturated to the point of hypertrophy, reawakens old memories of the Epicurean theory of simulacra found in Lucretius's *De rerum natura*. This was the theory that Simondon paid attention to when thinking about the cyclical becoming of images, about their iconogenesis. About those membranes or rinds detaching from the surface of bodies, Lucretius says that they "float [*volitant*] this way and that [*ultroque citroque*: i.e., hither and thither] through the air [*per auras*]." And he adds, further, that other simulacra exist that do not emanate from material bodies but are "spontaneously produced and self-created in the part of the sky that is called the air": "These, formed in countless ways, are swept along on high. Compare how sometimes we see clouds effortlessly massing together in the lofty heaven, marring the serene countenance of the firmament."[18]

We may also imagine that the flight of images staged in *The Battle of the Pictures* looks not just back to the past of antiquity but into the future, into today. What, in effect, is a flying image? What is that "aerial conflict" of images mentioned by the author of the first monograph about Hogarth, half a century after his death?[19]

Hogarth was obviously quite far from being able to imagine the extent to which our atmospheric space would become inhabited and would become, little by little, the theater of a true economic war both *of* and *for* images. The first aerial photograph that has been preserved is a view of Boston taken from a hot-air balloon by James Wallace Black on October 13, 1860, scarcely more than a century after *The Battle of the Pictures*. Writing in the *Atlantic Monthly*, the poet and doctor Oliver Wendell Holmes Sr. delights in the possibility of seeing a city "as the eagle and the wild goose see it," while Nadar, during these same years, dreams of exploiting "aerostatic photography" for military strategy and land surveys (he expects "a legitimate profit" from the latter).[20] Soon after the aerostat come the

18 Lucretius, *On the Nature of Things*, trans. Martin Ferguson Smith, pp. 101 and 104 (book IV, 31–2 and 131–6).

19 Clerk, *Works of William Hogarth*, p. 68.

20 Oliver Wendell Holmes, "Doings of the Sunbeam," *Atlantic Monthly*, July 1863, p. 12. James Wallace Black's photograph has been known by the title *Boston, as the Eagle*

Fig. 3.

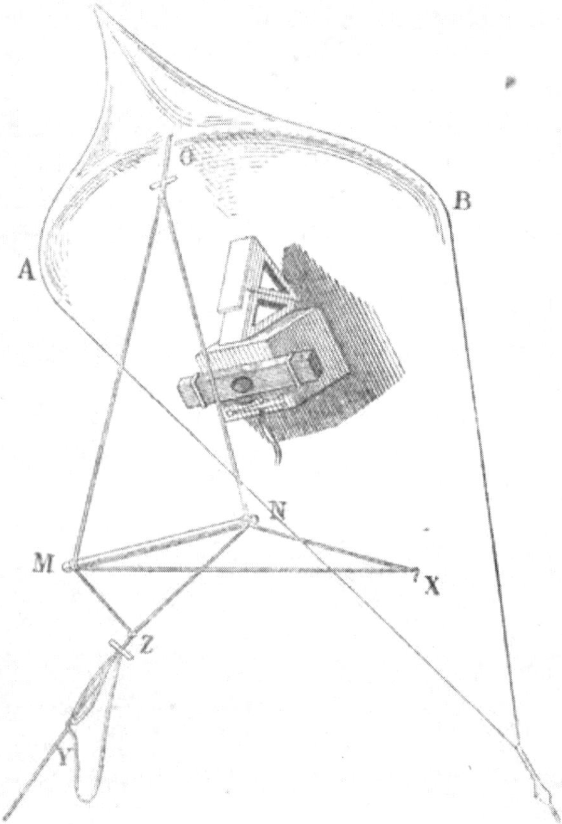

Schema of the kite, in Arthur Batut, La Photographie aérienne par cerf-volant *(Paris: Gauthier-Villars et fils, 1890).*

kites, equipped, in 1899, by the photographer Arthur Batut with a black box containing the film and a shutter released either by the combustion of a timing fuse or by electricity conducted along the metal kite strings.

Batut imagines increasing the available altitude of this flying viewpoint by sending up a series of kites linked one to the other:

> We'll launch an initial kite; and when it has reached the limit of the string it can bear, we'll attach its tip to the back of another kite; this second kite will rise up and extend the reach of the first, and we'll do this with a third kite and a fourth.[21]

With the later arrival of pigeon photography—the equipment for which was patented in 1907 by the German pharmacist Julius Neubronner—a large number of

---

and the Wild Goose See It (the Metropolitan Museum of Art owns a print). Nadar relates his attempts at aerial balloon photography in *When I Was a Photographer*, trans. Eduardo Cadava and Liana Theodoratou (Cambridge, MA: MIT Press, 2015), p. 61.

21 Arthur Batut, *La Photographie aérienne par cerf-volant* (Paris: Gauthier-Villars et fils, 1890), p. 48 (the first kite photograph is reproduced on the cover page). The sixth chapter, devoted to "the utility of aerial views," takes up Nadar's ideas (military strategy and land surveying) and adds both an exploratory and a recreational usage: "Anyone will be able to experience the illusion of a perilous ascent and contemplate the world from above without running any actual risk." We find the equivalent rhetoric around today's drones. In *The Story of the Earth's Atmosphere* (New York: D. Appleton, 1898), the British meteorologist E. Douglas Archibald claims to have used kites to photograph objects from above as early as 1887, but none of these snapshots seem to have been preserved.

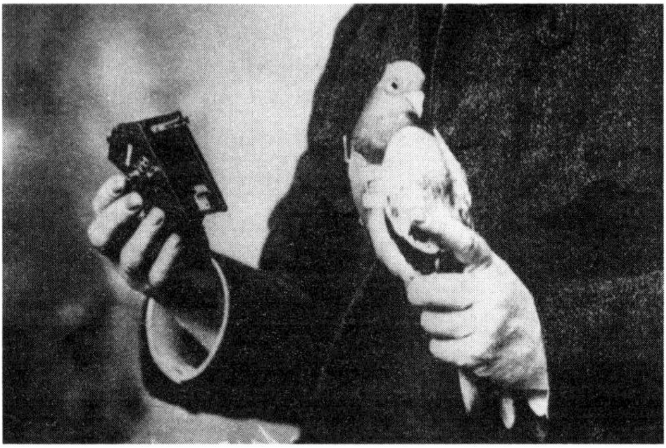

Photographic Camera Fitted Under the Belly of Pigeons, *1914 (Agence Rol, courtesy of Bibliothèque nationale de France, gallica.bnf.fr), detail.*

picture-takers began circulating in the skies. How different this was from the exquisite and overarching solitude that Nadar could still enjoy a few decades previously, during his first aerostatic ascents:

> Free, calm, levitating into the silent immensity of welcoming and beneficent space, where no human power, no force of evil, can reach him, man seems to feel himself really living for the first time ... he breathes, free from all the ties with this humanity which ends up disappearing in front of his eyes, so small even in its greatest achievements.[22]

---

22 Nadar, *Quand j'étais photographe*, p. 76. Julius Neubronner's patent was filed on June 21, 1907, and registered by the German Kaiserliches Patentamt under number 204721. See Fransziska Brons, "Bilder im Fluge. Julius Neubronners Brieftaubenfotografie," in *Fotogeschichte: Beiträge zur Geschichte und Ästhetik der Fotografie* 26, no. 100 (2006). The photograph

The cameras attached to homing pigeons, joining henceforth all those kites crisscrossing the skies, posed their own set of technical problems. Since the moment of the film's exposure could not be controlled by a human operator, a mechanism similar to Batut's timing fuse was required. The "chrono-shutter" (*Zeitverschluss*) built by Neubronner worked thanks to a pneumatic system: a ball of rubber, more or less filled with air, deflated at a rate that could be calculated in advance to correspond to the moment when the pigeon was supposed to arrive over the intended site.

While aviation gradually made obsolete these technologies over which we now cast a tender or nostalgic glance, atmospheric space was also becoming a sort of thoroughfare for those picture-takers placed on newer means of transportation that could cross the "Kármán line" (so called for the Hungarian physicist Tódor Kármán), which is the limit past which the atmosphere becomes too rarified to provide aerodynamic lift. The first photograph of Earth taken from extra-atmospheric space by a V2 rocket (number 13) dates from October 1946. And it was precisely one year earlier that the science fiction author Arthur C. Clarke had imagined that extraterrestrial space might become not only a privileged viewpoint to observe the earth but also a transportation network (along with undersea and underground cables) for the long-distance transmission of images. In a pioneering article titled "Extra-terrestrial Relays," Clarke—who gave Kubrick the idea for the monolith in *2001*—declares that in the future telecommunications will pass through a network of satellites

---

that Neubronner describes as "the first image made by a bird" is printed on p. 19.

(he imagines that three will be enough for global coverage).[23]

Since the launch of the first Soviet Sputnik—whose orbital trajectory interrupted a certain lecture of Heidegger's in 1957, two months after its launch—there are now over 6,000 satellites in orbit, according to the most recent data gathered by the European Space Agency.[24] Of these, 3,000 are still actually operational. This number, however, hides another: the tens of thousands of satellites launched into extra-atmospheric space from the beginnings of what we call "the space age" have also disseminated uncounted scraps of debris and junk (more than a million if we only consider those larger than a centimeter). The risk of collision—and so the exponential increase of these same debris causing such collisions—threatens to become uncontrollable.

Toward a Total Traffic Jam

To take the measure of what has happened to us with the advent of this extraterrestrial belt, adorned with ocular prostheses and crisscrossed by what could be called "eyeways," let's go back a bit and recall how Nadar, at

23 Arthur C. Clarke, "Extra-terrestrial Relays," *Wireless World* (October 1945), p. 306.

24 "Space Debris by the Numbers," European Space Agency, January 8, 2021, esa.int. Heidegger mentions Sputnik on several occasions in the three lectures that make up "The Nature of Language." See Martin Heidegger, *On the Way to Language*, trans. Peter D. Hertz (New York: Harper & Row, 1971), p. 62. The first of these lectures was given in Freiburg on December 4, 1957, two months to the day after the launch of the first artificial satellite on October 4.

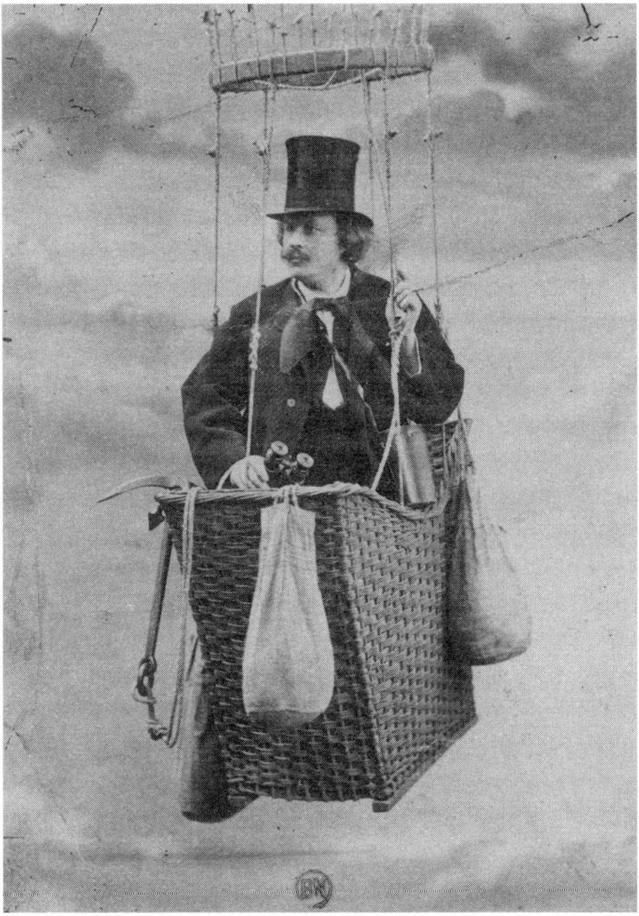

Nadar in a balloon (Nadar workshop, 1875–1895, courtesy of Bibliothèque nationale de France, gallica.bnf.fr).

the time of his stuttering attempts at aerial photography, speaks about the transmission of the pictures he took up there. Comparing his aerostatic viewpoint to "the bell tower of a village where a master sergeant can make his observations," he writes,

> I was carrying my bell tower with me and my lens was able, successively and indefinitely, to shoot positives on glass which I would send directly from my basket to the headquarters, by means of a very simple form of delivery (*factage*): a small box which would slide down to the ground through the length of a rope that would bring instructions back up to me, if necessary.[25]

The *factage*, or "lading," of images that Nadar is talking about—literally the transportation and delivery of his merchandise—takes a long time and requires rather labor-intensive handling. It is certainly lighter, though, than what Aby Warburg refers to as "the first, albeit colossal, automobile vehicle for images (*automobilen Bilderfahrzeug*)," that is to say the Flemish tapestry of the fifteenth century, which could be "freed from the wall" and carried elsewhere.[26] But the routing of images was still quite far from the apparent immediacy of their diffusion by satellite.

However, if we think about what this latter technology requires, the logistics and infrastructure involved

25 Nadar, *Quand j'étais photographe*, p. 79.

26 Aby Warburg, "The Absorption of the Expressive Values of the Past," trans. Matthew Rampley, *Art in Translation* 1, no. 2 (2009), p. 282; translation modified. In a 1907 article on Burgundian tapestry, Warburg proposes seeing it as "a mobile iconovehicle" (*ein bewegliches Bildervehikel*). Warburg, "Arbeitende Bauern auf burgundischen Teppichen," in *Gesammelte Schriften*, vol. 2 (Leipzig: B. G. Teubner, 1932), p. 223.

(satellites equipped with various microelectronics, their launch into orbit by rocket, the receptor dishes on the ground, the screens for viewing, not to mention the fossil fuel energy, rare earth metals, and all the other raw materials, along with the specialized assembly work required), then it starts to seem wholly contradictory to speak about "immediacy." "Immediate transmission" is in fact an oxymoron here. Of course, the temporality of the first aerial images was deferred both by the method of picture-taking (programmed by means of timing fuses) and by their mode of delivery (Nadar's "lading"). But far from simply disappearing, far from being reduced to nothing, this deferral is itself *deferred again*. We can never repeat enough that immediacy is generated by *deferring the deferral*, by means of ever more numerous technological mediations. This is so much the case that the immediate should really be thought of as a kind of thickening of the medium, a saturation rather than a distillation.[27]

In fact, the image supermarket in which we now live —this space swollen with images that *The Battle of the Pictures* anticipates—hides another logjam in those road networks of the visible that enable the circulation of the "automobile vehicles for images" theorized by Warburg. The transportation infrastructure along which our images circulate is decidedly choked up.

Up there, in what we too often imagine as a kind of immaterial and ethereal element, it's a complete traffic jam. Today, from his hot-air balloon, Nadar, raising his eyes skyward, would see cohorts and strings of satellites following each other, launched in their tens or hundreds

27 I have written on immediacy as an actual multiplication of mediation in *Supermarket of the Visible*, pp. 45–8.

(in the case of the Starlink project pursued by the firm SpaceX). It's a whole vehicular procession in orbit. Worse, the debris and metal scraps orbiting around the earth have formed an artificial asteroid belt, like wrecks and carcasses that, after the accident that made them, would continue to roll in the middle of traffic. Already in 1978, the astrophysicist Donald Kessler described the possible scenario for an orbital catastrophe that still bears his name (Kessler syndrome):

> As the number of artificial satellites in orbit increases, the probability of collisions between satellites also increases. Satellite collisions would produce orbiting fragments, each of which would increase the probability of further collisions, leading to the growth of a belt of debris around the earth.[28]

In a later article from 1991, Kessler imagines a growth in the satellite population such that various cleanup and removal companies will be required, a space-based sanitation department for those terrestrial excretions, which reminds us in turn of Bataille's wildest visions of the globe voiding its bowels in *The Solar Anus*.[29]

But it is not just orbital trajectories that this supersaturation threatens. It's not only above his head, in the starry heavens, that Nadar, in his floating nest, would see aerial traffic akin to terrestrial highways at peak

28 Donald J. Kessler and Burton G. Cour-Palais, "Collision Frequency of Artificial Satellites: The Creation of a Debris Belt," *Journal of Geophysical Research* 83, no. A6 (1978), p. 2637.

29 Bataille, "The Solar Anus" (1927), in *Visions of Excess*, ed. Allan Stoekl, pp. 5–9; Donald J. Kessler, "Collisional Cascading: The Limits of Population Growth in Low Earth Orbit," *Advances in Space Research* 11, no. 12 (1991), p. (12)63.

rush hour. All around him, atmospheric space, too, becomes congested with drones of civil and military use, which, in coming decades, are supposed to multiply even further. Patents have already been filed for delivery platforms akin to hives, while robotic technologies called "swarms" are under development for use both in the skies and elsewhere.[30]

Finally, there are those electromagnetic and radioelectric waves that bear images. Although they remain invisible, they traverse and saturate the atmosphere after the manner of Lucretius's simulacra. In the United States, the Federal Communications Commission began selling off—at auction—bandwidth frequencies used for fifth-generation mobile networks (5G), with download speeds a hundred times faster than those of the preceding generation. Similar auctions took place in France in 2020. As emphasized in a recent article in the British journal *Nature*, these frequencies are almost the same as those signals emitted by water vapor in the atmosphere, that is, the signals that are tracked by meteorological satellites. These satellites will now lose precision because of possible interference. The consequences are potentially grave—for instance, when trying to track the path of a hurricane.[31]

At the end of the evolution that leads from the "lading" of hot-air balloon photography to the heavy traffic of the satellites' eyeways and the contagion of electromagnetic frequencies, we come face to face with a paradox. That paradox can be articulated as a law

30 Patent filed by Amazon for the system baptized "Prime-Air." See Sam Levin, "Amazon Patents Beehive-Like Structure to House Delivery Drones in Cities," *Guardian*, June 26, 2017.

31 Alexandra Witze, "Global 5G Wireless Networks Threaten Weather Forecasts," *Nature*, April 26, 2019.

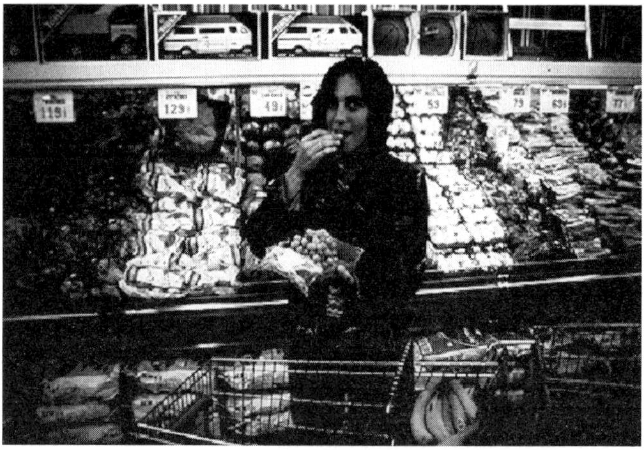

Supermarket, *Voyager golden record, 1977*
(courtesy of NASA, JPL-Caltech)

of iconomy or mediology: the more the aerial or celestial medium becomes saturated and thickened with the innervations that enable an immediate transmission, the more the medium's potential immediacy is threatened. Put another way: on the one hand, a medium is destined to become *immediate*, that is, immediately propagating of whatever it is mediating; but, on the other hand, the *immediation* of the medium, as a result of all these tracks beaten through it and all the traffic that cycles through them, leads the medium to reach its own limit and generate its own obstruction.

Filled space, space congested with images, of which *The Battle of the Pictures* gives us a foretaste, this iconomic space (which isn't far from being a "one hundred percent image space," as Walter Benjamin would say) appears to crystallize and solidify not only aboveground as well as underground or underwater (where cables run) but also in the atmosphere—inner and outer—becoming enveloped in a cloud of images and their vehicles, a saturated iconosphere that could well end up hindering, rather than helping, sight. Whereas the materialism of antiquity—of Epicurus interpreted by Lucretius—populated the atmosphere with the membranes and films of simulacra, a contemporary materialism must include among the elements of the iconosphere all those eyeway infrastructures that compose the woven texture of a visibility turned against itself.

Lost to Sight

Let us imagine that we could leave behind our terrestrial atmosphere, avoiding all those orbiting automobile vehicles for images, passing through the artificial asteroid belt of debris that seems to be on its way to forming a carapace around the earth. Imagine that we're following in the tracks of one of the two Voyager probes that were launched into deep space in 1977. Continuing their journey even now, they too carry images encoded in an analog format on a "golden record."[32] One of them depicts, in low resolution, a woman eating a bunch of grapes in front of the fruit and vegetable section in a supermarket. Who knows if she will be seen anew by someone or something else one day, out there, far away, so far?

---

32 Before the era of the digital image, NASA had developed a technique for image transformatting that we could summarize thus: the image is projected onto a screen; it is recorded with a TV camera, and the video signal is translated into sonic waves that can be engraved on a record. NASA engineers also included instructions for how to reverse this process so that the images might be read.

Let us imagine that the frame of *The Battle of the Pictures* has been blown up to the dimensions of an iconomy that contains the totality of an iconosphere both terrestrial and extraterrestrial. Let us imagine, then, that the particular flying image that seemed to want to run away from the others, the image that I proposed calling "iconofugal," had been thus launched at great speed toward the outer limits—but where might they be?—in this pictorial space amplified to the dimensions of the solar system or the universe itself. How far could it go? Perhaps its flight would take it toward a strictly iconomical excess, toward the visual overflow of a pure expenditure embodied in an image circulating at a speed that would surpass visibility. This would amount to an absolute speed differential in the field of the visible: an image whose "lading" or "automobile vehicle" could go faster than the speed of light.

In order to gain a sense of what this hypothetical scenario might look like, we could entrust ourselves to a literary fiction. To anyone skeptical of the relevance of such a move—choosing a text rather than visual materials to guide us—I would reply that the tale in question is not *merely* fictional, since it's inspired by contemporary astrophysics, and also that it attempts to locate the final frontier beyond which images are precisely no longer images, borne as they are toward their total eclipse in a state of pure loss.

Italo Calvino's short story titled "The Light-Years," in *Cosmicomics*, opens with the following epigraph that provides a narrative matrix:

> *The more distant a galaxy is, the more swiftly it moves away from us. A galaxy located at ten billion light-years from us would have a speed of recession equal to the*

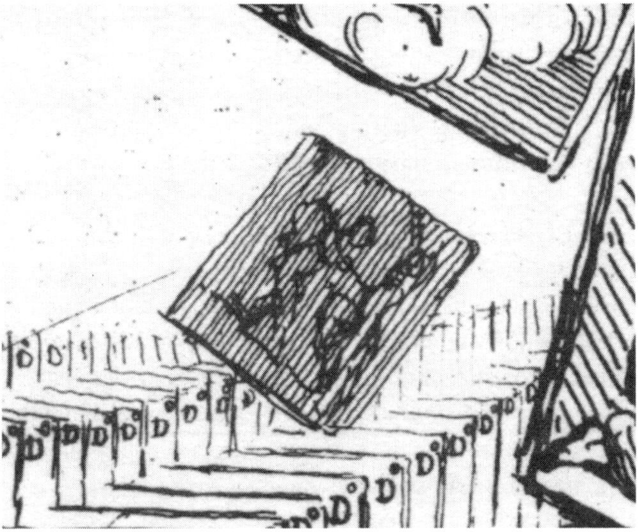

William Hogarth, The Battle of the Pictures, *engraving, 1745 (detail)*

speed of light, three hundred thousand kilometers per second.[33]

We have here a version of the theory known as "accelerated expansion of the universe" (although, to my knowledge, it hadn't yet been formulated in these terms when Calvino wrote the story). Researchers today have tried to prove the theory with the aid of cosmic "standard candles"—supernovae of the Ia type or cepheids—by comparing their theoretical luminosity with their luminosity when it reaches Earth, so as to calculate their distance as well as the speed at which they are traveling away from us. Numerous images gathered by

33 All quotations from Italo Calvino, "The Light Years," in *Cosmicomics*, trans. William Weaver (New York: Harcourt Brace Jovanovich, 1968).

NASA, thanks to the Hubble telescope, also appear to support the hypothesis of an accelerated expansion of the universe.

Calvino's introductory matrix serves to develop a truly hilarious scenario that begins like this:

> One night I was as usual observing the sky with my telescope. I noticed that a sign was hanging from a galaxy a hundred million light-years away. On it was written: I SAW YOU. I made a quick calculation: the galaxy's light had taken a hundred million years to reach me, and since they saw up there what was taking place here a hundred million years later, the moment when they had seen me must date back two hundred million years.

This proves very embarrassing for the narrator, since, he continues, "exactly two hundred million years before, not a day more nor a day less, something had happened to me that I had always tried to hide." The narrator is horribly ashamed of this action or accident "determined by exceptional conditions," and he has been waiting for oblivion to swallow it. This raises the question of what memory and oblivion could possibly mean at such a timescale, though the narrator says nothing about it. A witness is now able to testify to what he would have wished to repress or (if someone tried to dig into his past) deny.

Out of the reverberations of this shameful event unknown to the reader, Calvino's short story unfolds as an extraordinary iconomic meditation on the circulation of intergalactic messages that both relay and comment upon that event. The story meditates upon the speeds at which images and their traces that are marked out in recorded glances (the various "I SAW YOU") can be exchanged, round trip, in cosmic space. The first reflex (if we can speak about reflexes when it's a question of such lengths of time) of the one who was just caught in flagrante, so to speak (albeit a highly approximate way of speaking), is to respond with a sign of his own offering a promised explanation: "WAIT UNTIL I EXPLAIN." The wait here constitutes a temporal difference between what's promised (the explanation) and the fulfillment of that promise. But, here, this wait would also be redoubled by the wait for the message that says to wait, because the command "Wait" must also take time to arrive at its destination and the entity to whom it is addressed.

The narrator is well aware of this when he recounts his decision to ask for explanations himself instead of providing them:

> Before leaving myself open with any declaration I would have to know exactly what they had seen from the galaxy and what they hadn't: and for this purpose all I could do was ask using a sign on the order of DID YOU REALLY SEE EVERYTHING OR JUST A LITTLE BIT? or perhaps LET'S SEE IF YOU'RE TELLING THE TRUTH: WHAT WAS I DOING?, then I would have to wait long enough for them to be able to see my sign and then an equally long period until I could see their answer and attend to the necessary rectifications.

The delay required by the time it takes to see and be seen is thus amplified in totally hyperbolic fashion by the lengths introduced by this cosmic slo-mo with which something becomes visible. Never has anyone better illustrated how it takes time for anything to become apparent.

But—and here comes the most fascinating turn in the tale—the time until appearance, immensely stretched out as it is, is also differentiated: *the time of the image is deferred at the same time that it takes its time.* What I mean to say is that time stretches out as it flows. As the narrator says, taking note of the rigorous consequences of the accelerated expansion of the universe:

> All this would take another two hundred million years, or rather a few million years more, because while the images were coming and going with the speed of light, the galaxies continued to move apart, therefore that constellation now was no longer where I had seen it, but a bit farther on, and the image of my sign would have to chase it.

Taking the measure—if we may indeed speak of measures when confronted with the unmeasurable—of this sublime deferral, the narrator must renounce his hasty or premature solution (again an approximate way of speaking), a poorly thought-out solution that consisted simply in responding to the message, whether by offering or demanding explanations. Soon he also finds himself overwhelmed by the uncontrollable proliferation of images or of gazes that threaten to saturate the cosmic iconomy, just as they saturate the terrestrial iconomy: "The I SAW YOU sign, before I had glimpsed it, had certainly been read by inhabitants of other celestial bodies, and the same thing would have happened afterwards on the gradually more distant constellations." He fears that the "bad impression" he might have left during his "moment of heedlessness" would be "enlarged and multiplied, refracted across all the galaxies of the universe." It's a veritable iconomic nightmare that ends up clogging cosmic space: "In the nights that followed, I continued to see new signs with I SAW YOU on them, set on different constellations every time."

But beyond this universal narrator's hope, despair, dreams, and expectations, what is truly at play in the story is the notion of limit—a limit that is itself ever moving—beyond which there is no circulation or possible return, no more exchange of images. The narrator grieves when he foresees the moment when those most remote galaxies—with a rate of recession that also increases with their distance—would no longer be able to receive any of his messages:

> At a certain point the furthest galaxies that had seen me (or had seen the I SAW YOU sign from a galaxy closer to us, or the I SAW THE I SAW YOU from a bit further on) would reach the ten-billion-light-year threshold, beyond which they would move off at three hundred thousand kilometers per second, the speed of light, and no image would be able to overtake them after that.

What one has once seen—or seen as having been seen—out there would become "impossible to rectify": the image of the fatal moment, the snapshot of the original mistake, received immediately or mediately (the "I SAW YOU" or the "I SAW THE 'I SAW YOU'") would wander in those distant galaxies and "elude all further images"—"taking that now definitive image of me," the narrator adds, dismayed.

At this iconomic threshold that never ceases being displaced as the universe expands, we encounter the cosmicomic paradox—or better: the *cosmiconic* paradox—which is also a borderline state of the image: at its maximum speed of circulation, faster than light, the image becomes frozen by escaping us. Lost in every possible way, the image becomes fixed forever.

It is, of course, still an image, but one that never stops crossing or straddling the moving border beyond which it will be engulfed in the anoptic. This limit-image—this image at its own limits—is interwoven with the temporal differentials that are part of every image. But here, at this incessantly receding verge of which Calvino's cosmic iconomy is the theater, the temporal differentials inherent to the image involve more than transformatting (as in the case of Peter Schlemihl and his shadow) or the long durations that characterize the iconogenesis of living organisms (as in Simondon, Caillois, or Nabokov). What is at stake is the time of appearance itself, as it differentiates. And it's here that the image, toppling headlong in an excess of pure aniconomic expenditure, takes flight into total loss. It is lost to sight.